Strong Words 3

Strong Words 3

The best of the Landfall Essay Competition

Selected by Emma Neale
and Lynley Edmeades

OTAGO UNIVERSITY PRESS
Te Whare Tā o Te Wānanga o Ōtākou

Published by Otago University Press
Te Whare Tā o Te Wānanga o Ōtākou
533 Castle Street
Dunedin, New Zealand
university.press@otago.ac.nz
www.oup.nz

First published 2023

ISBN 978-1-99-004857-9

Published with the assistance of Creative New Zealand.

Design/layout: Fiona Moffat
Editor: Mel Stevens

Cover: *FrenchBayDarkly … #3*, John Reynolds, 2017, oil paint marker on acrylic on canvas, 152cm x 217cm.

Printed in New Zealand by Ligare.

Contents

EMMA NEALE

Open Fields

Two years after initial selection, each of the top five placed essays from the
Landfall 242 competition remains resonant and moving. Be it Andrew Dean's
eerie evocation of temporal fragility and the devastating freight of fascism;
Claire Mabey's fascination for 'the entanglement of time' and how our
perceptions of people can alter under the screen of habit or addiction; Susan
Wardell's quest for how to live as tauiwi on land with a violent colonial legacy;
Norman P. Franke's reflections on music as transcendence; or Susan Elliffe's
thoughts on how to grieve a lost friendship: the explorations in these works
gift readers a rich philosophical and psychological range. History is either
made vivid through sensory alertness or meditated upon with an academic
and erudite languor; in Dean's essay, it deftly wields both sensory and scholarly
modes. In one essay, a list delineates the struggle to marshal and control
emotional territory; in another, the focus hopscotches and darts with bright,
inquisitive, gleaming energy.

What strikes me most forcefully when I reread my 2021 choices is how
many of these writers take a central preoccupation and show the links and
reverberations that branch out from that heartwood towards multiple other
subjects, interests, experiences, possibilities. Under their hands, asides rarely
seem like digressions; instead, subtopics seem crucial to the process of
illumination.

A fuller discussion of the first five placed essays appears in *Landfall* 242.
In terms of this wider selection made for *Strong Words 3*, Rachel Buchanan's
'The Cares' strikes a singular note of difference both in its resolute focus and its
linguistic texture. The author unfolds the stresses of communicating with her
elderly mother, who has dementia, over Zoom during pandemic lockdowns.
It does so with a distancing, sometimes destabilising use of the second person,
'you', which at times speaks to the imagined reader, at times to Buchanan's

mother, and at others, gives a split, doubled-vision sense of the author talking to herself. Its sliding, scattered direction becomes a marker of emotional turmoil. The essay mixes in memoir, fantasy, extended metaphors, poetic parallelism, lists and nips of social history. Its often incomplete sentences are another stylistic marker of grief and of the way memory strobes and stutters in not always logically connected bursts. Its ending image of resignation and helplessness carries, through its incantatory structure, some of the emotional power of music.

'Through the Mist and into the Sunlight' by Alexis O'Connell might seem from its gentle title to deal with softer territory; yet its heading belies its rugged, heart-wrenching topic. The author records her experience as the only woman to run a half marathon with 'a group of broken [...] outcasts', the French Foreign Legion. As O'Connell recounts snippets of the 2008 race, her travels, and the local history of the French Occitanie region, she also delicately unfolds the psychological attrition that pushed her to take her children to France and try the running challenge.

O'Connell's skilful interweaving of personal experience and wider history is a quality she shares with several other writers in my selection, including Bonnie Etherington, whose 'A Fried Egg in Space' bravely and with a light touch documents diagnosis and surgery for a brain tumour. As she retells her experience, she also draws in comments on nuclear weapons manufacture, Covid, colonialism, ecological harm, and the paradoxical nature of language — that it can be both a means of grasping and yet also of potentially blocking an intimate understanding of place and biosphere. The essay itself is incontrovertible evidence of the author's determination and creative linguistic skills: qualities that serious illness so often stalks, shadows and undermines.

'Alchemy of the Airwaves', by Jayne Costelloe, is an anecdotal personal history that captivated my attention because of the vividness and energy of recall, and the taste of innocence. In an onslaught of often dark, bereft accounts in the overall submissions field, it felt like the tingle of health returning to cramped psychic spaces. It was a relief to know that someone, somewhere, recalled a happy childhood, felt moved enough to record it, and could do so without either dubious sentimentality or denial of natural frictions and frustrations. Are we not our joys and optimism as well as our dread, our wounds? We need the hard accounts; we need our writers and artists to expose the inequalities, the traumas, the injustices, the grief. But we also need to revive ourselves with song, with warmth, with love and connection. Otherwise, why are we here—and how do we go on?

Sarah Harpur Ruigrok, too, offers an antidote to loss and harm in her essay 'A Stand-up Mother': her comic flair was a rare, refreshing note in the entry field. Yet the humour is anything but frivolous, as it confronts social disapproval, hypocrisy, and a rhetoric of disdain for teen mothers. It laughs at the idea that one moral stance fits all situations and it exposes prurience disguised as concern. The essay also shows, I think, why comedy is so difficult to pull off and often uncomfortable in its mobile, febrile aim: sometimes, mid-laugh, we realise the joke might be on us. The essay casts its side-eye on classist, regionalist and sexist assumptions—and more. There are lines to make you laugh, reflect, and even want to talk back and argue. In a simple, fuss-free style, the author made me unsure which angle each new punchline or autobiographical fact would come from, nor which tonal style choice would undercut which. This gave her essay a tension and energy that confirmed its place in this selection, from a tough crowd of other, more somber possibles pushing from behind.

The etymology of 'essay' points us to the French for a trial, an attempt: the idea that even the final written piece is a provisional gesture. There is always more to be said, thought, discovered. It seems to me the term encodes the genre's own openness, its dual acknowledgment of effort and imperfection, and its constant striving for excellence. In the name's very acknowledgement of the ongoing need to explore and understand, to revisit and rethink, it also ensures its longevity as an art form. I think the robust health of the local variety, as shown here in *Strong Words 3,* cheers on that point resoundingly.

LYNLEY EDMEADES

Essay Lessons

The essay is having a moment in Aotearoa literature. Where writers were once told, 'essays don't sell', publishers in New Zealand are now issuing provisional contracts based on the reputation some writers may be gaining, largely from online publications. The personal aspect of the essay, or the 'personal essay', seems to be hitting buttons for writers and readers alike: we want to read stories of real people, we want to know what people think and feel, what they're struggling with and what makes them tick.

The personal essay is, like observational comedy, concerned primarily with just that—observation—and largely through the lens of the subjective. While personal essays might be funny and entertaining, satirical and incisive—and often very accurate—I must admit they regularly leave me wanting. As Merve Emre recently wrote in *The New York Review of Books*, the personal essay is 'the genre whose formal conventions—the "capital I" of "I think" or "I feel"—not only draw the individual into public view, but also insist upon the primacy of the individual.' The self as subject; the subject as self. Whether the turn towards the individual—as exemplified in this particular essayistic mode—is largely driven by identitarian politics is the subject of another introduction, perhaps.

While all the essays in this selection for *Strong Words* are engaged with, or interested in, the 'personal', what enlivens them is that they're not limited to that characteristic. The essays that demanded a second, third and fourth reading were those that felt to me to shirk this 'primacy of the individual' somewhat. These essays tend to use the self as the starting point, rather than the subject; they look instead to the self *in-the-world*, so to speak. And in doing so, they exhibit not only the observations of a mind but the process of the mind *doing* the observation. They *are* personal in their reflections, but they also display the process of doing, of the mind engaging with ideas and trying to work through things. 'The hero of the essay,' writes William Gass, 'is its author in the act of thinking things out, feeling and finding a way; it is the mind in the marvels and miseries of its makings, in the *work* of the imagination, the search for form.'

It is this 'search for form' that also enables great essays to aspire to something more akin to the poem. In his 'Ars Poetica', Archibald MacLeish writes that 'a poem should not mean/But be.' The poem should *perform* its meaning, rather than simply offer a reflection on that meaning or message. This is not to say great essays are incomplete or loose, or that they follow a kind of stream of consciousness. Quite the opposite. The best essays are both waterproof and leaky, crafted and open. They 'shy away from the violence of dogma', in Theodor W. Adorno's words; they don't profess to know everything or to have mastered their subjects. They don't aspire to a sense of completeness or conclusion. Instead, the essay opens and expands, inclining *towards* an understanding, but where the 'inclining' is the driver or the plot.

The introduction-as-genre obliges me to say something about the essays that follow. Rather than offer single-sentence conclusions about each piece before slotting them all comfortably (or uncomfortably) into clusters of topics, I will try to say something about the selection as a whole. The subject matter varies widely, and each essayistic approach is so wildly different that making comparisons and forming clusters feels like comparing an apple to a bookshelf. And yet, I see one thread that (loosely) ties all these essays together: learning. Our narrators are all engaged in the act of learning: how to start using 'they' as their personal pronoun (see 'Securitising Gender' by Jessica Ducey); that they've got breast cancer, and that this cancer is the result of overwork which is the result of post-colonial trauma (see 'Lumpectomy' by Tina Makereti); how to speak Cantonese (see 'Reasons to Learn Cantonese' by Maddie Ballard); how to play a Nick Cave song on the guitar (see 'This Dark Country' by Claire Mabey); how to shuck oysters, which is really a way of learning that the land they have grown up calling their own has never belonged to them (see 'How to Shuck an Oyster' by Charlotte Doyle). What connects all of these—and possibly what drew me to select them— is their openness. The act of learning—and performing this learning in the essay itself—implies an acknowledgement of the flabby, leaky and largely unknowable world beyond the self. There is a spirit of *wow, look at this*, a recognition that we cannot—personally and collectively—hold all the world in our minds.

In a time of increased drive for totality and mastery, engorged with greed and possessiveness, to say *I'm still learning* feels like an act of anarchy. It is anarchic in form: the essay as ongoing, incomplete, leaky and open, grounded by its not-knowing-ness. But it is also anarchic in its subject matter, like a new form of confession: *I don't know (anything; everything; the answers)*. It admits that we're not in control, and that to aim for control—and I'm thinking here of the environment—is a crapshoot we should have given up on decades ago. It also offers something of an antidote to the quickfire, combative nature of social media, where binaristic opinions are the modus operandi. They offer a rich alternative to the evidence-based, data-driven hyper-capitalism that tries to mop up every aspect of our daily lives. Self-confessed supposition combined with a good dose of curiosity in the unknown is the essayistic mode par excellence.

These essays, in their various acts of learning, suggest we need to try and work *with*, rather than *in spite of*. The essay is a place to pay attention to the self—the self in the world, and, more importantly, the world beyond the self.

REFERENCES

T.W. Adorno, 'The essay as form', trans. Bob Hullot-Kentor, *New German Critique* 31, Spring–Summer, 1984.

Merve Emre, 'The illusion of the first person', *New York Review of Books*, vol. LXIX, no. 17, 3 November 2022.

William Gass, 'Emerson and the essay', *Habitations of the Word* (Simon and Schuster, 1985).

Archibald MacLeish, 'Ars Poetica', in *Collected Poems 1917–1952* (Houghton Mifflin Harcourt, 1952).

ANDREW DEAN

The New Man

I moved to east London in early autumn 2018 following the hottest summer in a decade. I'd had one last valedictory season in Oxford: long evenings in the garden, punting on the Isis, cricket in the fading light. By September, the leaves were beginning to turn, and my long-delayed departure began.

In May I had signed a lease for a room in a shared flat in London. The whole place would be renovated over the summer, I was told. The owners had initially promised that the work would be done in a couple of months, by August at the latest. After the deadline passed they told me they needed more time. September came and went. By early October, when I eventually moved in, the carpet was yet to be laid, and all of the rooms—except mine—were piled floor to ceiling with unassembled parts of a house. There was plasterboard in the living room, timber in a bedroom, cushions and pieces of chairs in the bathtub.

In the building site beyond my room, nothing worked. Turning on the kettle would plunge the living room into darkness. The washing machine's spin cycle cut power to the downstairs flat.

Gurgles and watery clanks sounded through the night. At first the noises came from my radiator, but soon they were coming from somewhere deeper, harder to determine. I'd wake up to a heave, a clank—and then silence. One evening in November, sections of the kitchen ceiling fell in, spreading a fine layer of dark grey dust over the floor and bench.

In those first few weeks in London, I would wake each morning to find teams of labourers in the house. The beginning of the day's work would be heralded by Polish folk ballads. The workers would stay all day, hammering and shouting, smoking out the window. About twice a week a man named Marion would come in the later evening, after all the other men had left. He would work until two or three in the morning, Radio Three playing from his plaster-spattered stereo. One night, against the lamplight, he told me that today was the second anniversary of his wife's death. This was difficult to recall, he said, not only because she was the only woman he had ever loved, but also because their son had undergone a mental collapse following his mother's death, and had spiralled into drugs and crime. The son was now in prison in Romania, he said. I didn't ask after his daughter. He told me she had recently been disabled.

Marion's struggles did not help the air of unreality that had settled over my life. Between the rubble, the ballads, the leaks, the plasterer's ghosts and everything else, I had the sense that nothing was quite as it was, or should be. Perhaps if I went upstairs to the empty shell of the loft, I thought, I would just slip across to the other side. There would be one great clank, the power would go out again, and that would be it for me.

Almost imperceptibly, though, the other world that had opened up before me began to close itself off. The renovations were completed (if never quite finished), the carpet was laid, and the plumbing and electrics were fixed. A new washing machine was installed. I heard fewer Polish folk songs, and then eventually none at all. The last I saw of Marion was his departing figure after he pushed the keys through the mail slot.

I assembled pieces of furniture from around the house until I had something like a bedroom. There were reminders of the time just past—pencil marks on walls, unpatched holes in the ceiling—but it seemed as though those odd few weeks were behind me. Another life, which had felt so close, slipped out of mind.

*

It was in October that I first cycled along Cable Street. This is the East End proper: the skyscrapers of the City of London nearby dominate the squat council flats of Whitechapel. I had come here because my father's family had lived around Cable Street between the wars—or so I had been told. They had been part of the extraordinary mass exodus of Jews from the Pale of Settlement in Eastern Europe that took place in the five decades from around 1880. Escaping persecution and pogroms, Russian Jews moved all over the world, to the United States in particular. Around 150,000 went to London. By one estimate there were more than 200,000 Jews in London in the 1930s, most of whom lived in the East End.

What little I knew of that generation of émigrés was filtered through my father's half-told stories. His maternal grandparents, Harry and Jane Wislaw, were in the schmatte trade. Harry was a tailor, Jane a seamstress. This was a common line of work for Jews at the time: immigrants in the slums of London's inner east performed the labour of Savile Row. After the war, Harry and Jane left behind a bombed-out Britain to live out the remainder of their lives in suburban Christchurch, New Zealand. For my father's bar mitzvah they gave him a bicycle. His stories of them end around then. About my father's paternal grandparents, I knew little other than what I could intuit from my grandfather's contemptuous asides.

Wandering around those streets, past estate agents and off-licences, I couldn't find anything that matched my image of how life might have been here between the wars. Whatever sense I had was probably formed by my memory of a single photograph of my father's early life in Britain. It's black and white, and he's being wheeled in a pram down a London street. Everyone looks cold. It might be winter—or this might just be what England is like. In the background are a few trees and a detached house.

It began to dawn on me, here among the council flats, that the stand-alone house suggested that the photograph was probably not taken in London after all. Villas and bungalows are more the terrain of my father's later home in Westminster Street, Christchurch. What I thought was the postwar chill may well have been the breeze blowing in from the Pacific.

My memory-work was doomed from the outset, of course. This part of London has been serially made over in the waves of destruction and construction that mark modern British history: the Blitz, inflows and outflows of migration, Thatcher, and the tentacular growth of the City. Any traces that could have remained would almost certainly have been made over and then made over again in this cycle of demolition and rebuilding.

Few Jews remain in the East End now. After the war, with much of the area destroyed by German bombing, most moved northwest, to neighbourhoods such as Golders Green. Some emigrated, including Harry and Jane. Newer arrivals, largely from Bangladesh, settled in the East End in the 1960s and 1970s. Where there were once 150 active synagogues in this area, there are now four.

What was I doing here? It should have been obvious that I wouldn't find traces of interwar life hidden in the brickwork, and not only because of everything that had happened in the intervening decades. In reality, I knew next to nothing about the figures whose steps I thought I might be retracing. I had never even seen photographs of them. All I had were my father's recollections, vague and sometimes painful, which shimmered into and out of significance. He used to call his grandparents from a phone box in front of a cemetery on Grahams Road, Christchurch. His bicycle was stolen from outside the hospital soon after their deaths. Their graves were in Linwood Cemetery. Harry ate little other than steamed fish. They argued in Yiddish.

Leaving behind the council flats, I searched for something that I knew definitely was on Cable Street. Near Shadwell Station there is a mural several storeys high, covering one end of a row of terraces. It commemorates the 'Battle of Cable Street', the anti-fascist demonstrations against Oswald Mosley's Blackshirts in October 1936. Mosley's 3000 Blackshirts were met by 50,000 protesters, and somewhere between 100,000 and 300,000 more further along the route. Despite attempts by police to clear the way, the march was eventually abandoned.

The mural depicts a city street in ferment. Police horses charge protesters while packed crowds fight the massed authorities. Banners are flying, bodies are captured in motion, and pieces of machines wheel through the crowd. Above, residents hurl rubbish from the upper windows—glass bottles, propaganda leaflets and the contents of chamber-pots.

It was the Jewish presence in the East End that had turned it into a target for the growing fascist movement in Britain in the later 1920s and 1930s. Mosley formed the British Union of Fascists (BUF) in 1932, and it quickly became the nation's largest extreme right-wing group. In November 1933 a front-page article in the BUF's newspaper announced details of the Jewish conspiracy against Britain.

The *Daily Mail* in January 1934 ran the headline 'Hurrah for the Blackshirts', under the name of the newspaper's owner, Viscount Rothermere. The immediate prelude to the events of October 1936 was a campaign of hooliganism led by the BUF and other affiliated groups, including window-smashing and attacks on Jewish-owned shops. Street violence that targeted Jewish residents had become common in the East End by this time.

While the Battle of Cable Street ended in defeat for the BUF, it led to a further radicalisation of the far right. BUF meetings swelled in the East End.

Mick Clarke, a local fascist leader, declared at one meeting: 'London's pogrom is not very far away now. Mosley is coming every night of the week in future to rid East London and by God there is going to be a pogrom!'

In going to Cable Street, I was undertaking my own minor version of heritage tourism. But my trip was ultimately less about looking for what I might find than it was about looking for what might no longer exist. I couldn't seriously expect, here in the East End, to find the place my family had left. Another way of putting it is that there's no East End for me to find. Discovering what you left behind is not the kind of thing that happens to my father's family, to Jews. There's no family farm, no little church or village shop. The temple was destroyed and, much later, a homeland invented. I went home and picked up a curry on the way.

*

To support a new research project on Jewish comedy, my job in London came with few formal responsibilities. I quickly found the autonomy to be a mixed blessing, however, as I had little idea where I was going with my work. As is typical with academic positions, I had been hired on the strength of what I had just finished rather than what I would now be starting. The two-year contract was too short to require tangible results, but too long to ignore that prospect outright. My manager's expectations were opaque, communicated mainly through raised eyebrows and extended pauses. *And what are you planning to work on next?*

I slowly came to understand that my project was unlikely ever to be completed. The topic *could* appeal to me, but I didn't know how to write something new about it. It was too vast, too well covered, and anyway, I probably didn't have the skills. I don't speak Yiddish, and my knowledge of Jewish biblical material is negligible. I never actually announced this thought to myself or anyone else, but my habits nonetheless began to organise themselves around it, like water around a rock. Month by month, my working hours became shorter and my weekends longer. I went to Venice three times in the spring and played cricket midweek in the summer.

I took to haunting the British Library, rummaging through its catalogues. In this purposelessness masquerading as research I consulted joke books, pamphlets and tracts, newspapers, histories of comedy, histories of Jews and anti-Semitism in Britain. For a brief moment I thought about trying to learn Yiddish—then booked myself another holiday.

One of the far-right tracts I read was *The Alien Menace*, published in five updated editions between 1928 and 1934. Written by Lieutenant-Colonel A.H. Lane, each edition of the book raises alarm about recent immigration. In the first, just under a hundred pages in length, Lane writes: 'This book might be called "Britain for the British"'. What follows is a heady mix of racial pseudo-science and decreasingly veiled anti-Semitism. In his preface he claims that recent migrants are 'generally the scum of Central and Eastern Europe'. This is 'not intended to be anti-Jewish,' he says, but rather 'anti-alien and pro-British'.

Over time, in line with the radicalisation of anti-Semitism in Britain, Lane became more virulent in his denunciation of Jews. One of his central claims was that Jews are at the origins of the scourge of international communism. He repeatedly refers to Karl Marx as 'the Prussian Jew'. He says that Bolshevism is 'controlled by a combination of internationalists in which those of the Jewish faith predominate'.

Paradoxically, Jews are also ruthless capitalists. He worries that 'our most important industries … are now wholly or partly controlled by German American Jewish interests'. Jews, we discover across the fifth and final edition's 250 pages, are all of these things at once: politically powerful and physically degenerate, exploitative controllers of capital, ruthless communists and impoverished vectors of disease, directing the media yet curiously unable to be viewed kindly by the ordinary British man.

Reading such tracts was both amusing and banal. In time, I became immune to the claims the authors were making. It was as though their rhetorical strategies had been forced through a mincer. As I confronted a mush of rhetoric day after day, the writing became uniform, a series of gestures that amounted to the same thing—another claim that Jews run the world, that the body politic is withering away, that 'we' are on the brink of a race war, that Jews use Christian blood for matzo.

I read deeply into the appendices of *The Alien Menace*. With Lane's army career now behind him, he had the time to assemble a list of newspaper cuttings that reported immigrant crimes. Each new threat indicates yet another moral crisis: from 'Deportations' and 'Illegal Landings, etc.' to 'Thefts, etc.' and

'Fraudulent Trading, Bankruptcies'. Alongside my fair-minded guide, I learnt to be as worried about 'International Thieves and Swindlers' as about those foreign-run centres of vice, 'Opium Dens, Night Clubs, etc.'

One case in *The Alien Menace*, under 'Passports, etc.', caught my eye. On 1 January 1927 the *Daily Mail* reported that a man who had gone by numerous different names, 'an electrical engineer of no fixed address', had been convicted of 'entering the country with an irregular passport and stealing a passport'. He was said by the prosecution to be 'a runner or messenger for the Communist Party'. His sentence was six months' imprisonment and a recommendation for deportation. The clipping contained a brief biography:

> [He] registered in England as a Russian in the name of Neumann in 1916. Neumann was believed to be his correct name. In 1918 he appeared to have gone to America, and in 1924 returned to London, living in the East End. During the general strike last May he was very active. When that was over he left the East End and went to live with a friend named Prowse at Tottenham, N. Last June he stole Mr Prowse's passport, and travelled on the Continent with it. Last year he bought a passport for 500 francs from a Frenchman, and went with it to Germany and Holland, and last Friday arrived at Harwich.

> Detective-Sergeant Foster, of Scotland Yard, said that [he] had used the names of Gurowitz, Neumann, Newman, Caquin, and Prowse. He had tried to become naturalized in America.

Lane was presumably drawn to this case for several reasons. The first is the series of lies the man told about his identity. This menace had slid in and *lived among us*. The second is the suggestion that this man was Jewish—several of his names, along with his origins, and where he had lived in London, imply as much. The time of his arrival, for Lane, also showed his cowardice. The man was probably seeking to avoid conscription into the Tsarist army, and Russia was a British ally for the first three years of the war and a bulwark against communism. Finally, and worst of all, are his political leanings (which of course confirm his Jewishness). His actions during the General Strike, and his decision to clear out of the East End afterwards, show that he was involved in fomenting trouble on behalf of Judaic class warfare. A lying, rootless, disloyal, communist Jew.

What was I looking for at the British Library? If I had come looking for the remnants of my family, Neumann is as close to an adoptive ancestor as could be imagined—a Jewish everyman at the moment of crossing over. In the blurred outlines of this man's story I saw shimmering into view a figure of the many human lives that lie behind the great historical forces of the century. He seems to float on the winds of the era: persecution, war, emigration, exile, Bolshevism, strikes. A person with no apparent source of income and no clear past, he had been blown about in the madness of a world that had lost its mind. A new man, washed clean both of and by history.

There is a word in Yiddish for the kind of character Neumann was: luftmensch, a man who lives on air. A luftmensch can come from anywhere and with any purpose: a criminal or a cod-philosopher; an organ-grinder or a down-on-his-luck businessman; a dubious inventor or a tramp. He is as likely to turn up to a Seder in rags as he is to arrive wearing a gold watch. He may never be heard of again or he may be impossible to get rid of. The *Guardian* reported that when Neumann arrived in Britain from France, he presented himself to immigration officers as 'an electrical engineer'. He said that 'he had come to this country to put a new blowlamp on the market. He was unable to speak a word of French and had no papers on him relating to any blowlamp'.

There was an odd coda to Neumann's story, which I discovered in the fragile collections of the British Library's newspaper reading room. It seems that he or someone close to him later told the *Sunday Worker* that the police had attempted to 'extort' a confession from him. The newspaper reported:

> *He has been on a bread-and-water diet. His cell is in a filthy condition, and he is not allowed a mattress, but has to sleep on the floor. No doubt this is intended to make him more amenable to the third degree inquisition.*

Despite these conditions, Neumann still found time to send 'fraternal greetings to the Workers, both British and Chinese, who are struggling for the overthrow of capitalism'.

The *Sunday Worker's* accusations of police heavy-handedness led to a libel case against its editor, which the police eventually won. It turned out that the police had no access to Neumann's cell and that the prison regime was no different for him than it was for anyone else. This electrical engineer had been detained as little more than an ordinary thief. As a later retraction noted: '[T]he statements in the original paragraph were quite unjustified'.

What became of this luftmensch, this man of air? He was never deported, despite the court's recommendation. He went on to have ten children in England, who went by some of the many names Neumann adopted. I have every reason to believe that one of the children was Lionel Dean, my paternal grandfather. While I will never be certain, there are enough parallels in the reporting on Nathan Neumann—name, job, origin, year of arrival—to suggest that he was in fact the luftmensch paterfamilias. Some of my cousins are named Newman, although they've discussed returning it to what they believe to be the original family name, Neumann. Then there are the Deans, of whom I am one. There may well be some Caquins, Prowses and Gurowitzes out there.

There has always been some unspecified hint of scandal in my family associated with Lionel's father. Lionel didn't say much about him, other than that he was no good. *No good* was in fact one of my grandfather's phrases. It was never that clear to me what he meant by this—a shirker, a scrounger, a liar, a luftmensch. *My father?* he would say. *No good.*

*

The only time I have visited the graves of my father's other grandparents, Harry and Jane Wislaw, was when I was in Christchurch on a book tour to give a talk about nostalgia in politics. I asked the audience: what might it mean to be living in the past? Are we in a romance with what can never be called back, and with what might never have existed? Whenever the audience tried to steer me back to politics I found myself speaking embarrassingly from the heart. We only know what we want from what we once wanted, I told them, as I felt myself slipping into another life entirely: when I feared harm and took shelter in my parents' arms. My editor, sitting in the front row, looked vaguely alarmed.

I had been out with my parents to the Linwood Cemetery, on the east side of Christchurch, before the talk. Both my parents have relatives buried here, on different sides of the cemetery. The graveyard is a record of early colonial immigration, the plots split into different religions (separated even in death). On the south side, with a view back towards the city, are the grand nineteenth-century headstones of the early Anglicans. Halfway up the hill, to the northwest and near a major road, are the Catholics.

Most of the graveyards in Christchurch were damaged in the earthquakes of 2010 and 2011. On Linwood's sandy ground the land had warped, lifted and dropped thousands of times, flattening headstones and breaking open tombs. The monument to Thomas Dixon (beloved husband of Janet, d. 1918) lay in three pieces next to his distended concrete grave—the pillar, the capital and the rounded stone decoration. The tomb of Clara Clark (d. 1906, beloved wife of W.H. Clark) lay on its side.

There are few visible signs of Jewish life in Christchurch. This is a city in which the spire of the cathedral was once visible from kilometres away in every direction. However, in Linwood, a series of low monuments, all in black, record the presence of Jews from the settlement's early history—Friedlanders, Schwartzes and Woolfs.

It will always be a shock to see the Star of David in suburban Christchurch. Whatever led these people to come to the end of the earth was much like whatever led Neumann to leave Russia. It was part of the same historical process. My father, who was with me, stopped in front of the grave of Harry Teplitzky (d. 1977, immigrated 1920). 'Oh,' he said. 'Tip.'

Eventually we found my father's maternal grandparents. The flat stones were undamaged. Harry Wislaw (d. 1965, immigrated 1953), a tailor. Jenny Wislaw (d. 1970, immigrated 1953), a seamstress, known as 'Jane'. A Star of David with simple text on a black background. We placed pebbles on the graves and waited in the autumn breeze for something to happen.

Amid all the destruction, none of the Jewish graves had been disturbed. The monuments here are simpler, hidden away, less vulnerable to shaking. They face a different direction, from east to west. For once, here in Christchurch, the Jews had been left undisturbed.

TINA MAKERETI

Lumpectomy

For a while, I call her Frankenboob. After surgery, she has three gnarly scars, if you count the one in the armpit where the sentinel lymph nodes were removed, which I do, plus another lighter mystery wound where something else happened, who knows what. She is also bright blue in one big patch, from the radioactive substance they injected to find the sentinel nodes—a sentence I can't write without thinking of *The Matrix*. Much later, when I'm beginning radiotherapy, they explain there are titanium clips throughout Frankenboob too, placed there by the surgeon to indicate where cancer has been, or is likely to develop, so they can boost the area with extra beams of targeted radiation if they deem it necessary, which they do, since I am young. One of the surprise benefits of cancer is how often people tell me I'm young. The oncologist and the registrar share an affectionate giggle when they note how blue my breast remains several weeks after surgery. They are both immigrant women, and I'm pleased to be in their company. This is what women can do, no matter where we're from, laughing about a blue boob—with no men to concern us.

It started, as it always does, with a lump. And then a mammogram, which showed nothing untoward, according to the attending doctor. It was the technician doing the follow-up ultrasound who identified some problematic masses, which meant she had to consult with the mammogram doctor, and he had to have a feel. Having started the day thinking the appointment was going to be routine, I hadn't shored myself up for some invasive touching, so it was deeply alarming, but at subsequent visits, I get used to it. The appointments always go like this: Can I feel it? Did a mammogram find it? Did you find it? No, I always reply, the mammogram didn't find it. Yes, it was me. No, I wasn't doing a routine check. Maybe I was showering, or tweezing or something, I can't remember. One day it was just there.

'We always do a biopsy when we find masses like this,' the mammogram doctor said, in such a reassuring way that I assumed everything was fine. By this point I was pretending very hard that nothing was happening anyway, so I quietly chose to ignore the technician's expression.

At the time, it seemed unlikely. No one in my family has had breast cancer. I breastfed two children for nearly two years each, smug in the knowledge that this would decrease the likelihood of getting it. In 2020, I spent a large amount of money on an integrative medical doctor who conducted a barrage of tests to try to pinpoint the cause of my chronic stress and ongoing fatigue (aside from, you know, work). We tested my blood and my breath and my poop, re-engineered my diet and took inventory of my life from birth. There were some red flags in that, to be sure, but no cancer.

For a few days, I went on with my life. I was too busy to worry. Then my GP called and left a message in a sad voice saying she was there if I wanted to discuss anything. She ended the call with 'I hope you're okay.' I was suddenly, alarmingly, not okay. I called her back, and she patiently answered my questions, both of us somewhat concerned that the mammogram doctor hadn't made it clear that there were definitely Things To Worry About. A day or so later I received the first report of many via the Manage My Health website. 'Findings here are probably malignant', it said for one lesion, 'this is also suspicious for malignancy' it said for the other. Despite my propensity for optimism and my denial that this could possibly be happening, I knew it was unlikely to be wrong.

'I love my breasts,' women with breast cancer often say when explaining their decision to seek breast-conserving surgery or to have reconstructive surgery. I know that one of the reasons I found it hard to imagine that I had breast cancer, one of the reasons I wasn't entirely sure I believed it even when I was having treatment for it, is that my breasts have been, on the whole, benevolent: forces for good, not evil; nurturing not only children but relationships and body image and identity. Long before I ever contemplated the possibility of losing my own breast(s), I found that Tig Notaro joke hilarious, the one she made after her double mastectomy, about how her breasts got sick of her making jokes about their size and decided to kill her. How else do we come to terms with murderous breasts, but to laugh?

*

At the biopsy appointment, the specialist pulled up the imaging of my breast from the previous appointment and was helpfully definitive. 'This is a very clear cancer,' he said, circling an area on the screen, 'and it looks like there's a smaller one here you wouldn't have been able to feel.'

Well, that's it, I thought. Tears came then, just a few, rolling quietly down my face. I reached for my husband's hand. The specialist and specialist nurse waited patiently. They must see this every single day, I thought. 'You did well catching it—it's very early,' the specialist said. I will be told this often, and I certainly felt the truth of it. Nothing else would be conclusive until more tests and surgery and testing of what they removed during surgery, but because we'd found it early this kind of cancer usually had high chances of survival—85 to 95 percent over five to ten years. But I hadn't yet contemplated the possibility of nonsurvival.

The rest of the appointment was somewhat jolly. The surgeon made fun of my profession and my parenting decisions as he used ultrasound to pinpoint my malignancies and inserted massive needles with scissory tips to snip a bit of flesh for the biopsies. I was up for the teasing, tried to give as good as I got. Anything but pity. My husband focused on breathing and not looking. 'Sympathetic nervous response,' the surgeon said, nodding towards him, 'It's often the husbands who have stronger reactions'. We both averted our eyes, but the needles were long enough to flash into my peripheral vision anyway, and despite the blissful numbness brought on by the local, there was a lot of prodding and shoving.

'There's quite extreme variation in the density of women's breasts,' the specialist nurse told us. She was very good at explaining everything that happened. 'Some are like butter and some are like rubber car mats.' The implication was that mine fall towards the rubber mat end of the spectrum.

The test results were 'good', by which I mean non-surprising, by which I mean that it was definitely the big C, but it wasn't nastier than we had anticipated. I had the most common form of breast cancer, hormone-positive, 'easy' to treat. The thing to do was cut it out, and once they'd cut it out, the cancer would be gone, even though the conditions that caused the cancer would still be there. Most of the time, they dealt with that by 'sanitising the area' with radiation, or a systemic approach using drugs. It was likely that I wouldn't need chemotherapy, thank all the gods. And then the medical intervention would be done, even though the conditions that caused the cancer might still be there.

*

I was completely surprised, and yet I was wholly unsurprised. Life is paradoxical —grittily, hungrily, wonderfully and painfully so—and an utter mystery. The mystery that found me in February 2021 said, so, cancer huh? What's that about? Within weeks of my diagnosis, I discovered Dr Gabor Maté's *When the Body Says No* and was relieved to find that my gut feeling about what was going on had some scientific backing. As Maté describes:

> *Women with a history of breast cancer were asked what they thought had caused their malignancy. Forty-two per cent cited stress—much more than other factors such as diet, environment, genetics and lifestyle … No other cancer has been as minutely studied for the potential biological connections between psychological influences and the onset of the disease. A rich body of evidence, drawn from animal studies and human experience, supports the impression of cancer patients that emotional stress is a major contributing cause of breast malignancy.*

Maté notes that women are rarely asked about this aspect of their lives in treatment. This was my experience. In fact, that first specialist had a good old laugh when I tried to explain how overwhelmed I was by work. I teach at a university, and my work is in arts and creativity, which in my opinion is essential for life but must be quantifiably less stressful than, say, medicine or law, so even I am a bit confused about why it gets so stressful. Compulsive overwork is a habit in academia, almost a requirement, and few of us say no. Although there is more to it. Says Maté:

> *Research has suggested for decades that women are more prone to develop breast cancer if their childhoods were characterized by emotional disconnection from their parents or other disturbances in their upbringing; if they tend to repress emotions, particularly anger; if they lack nurturing social relationships in adulthood; and if they are the altruistic, compulsively caregiving types.*

I could tick all of those boxes, at one point or another. And 2020 turned into a particularly toxic year at work. In the three years leading up to 2020, it wasn't unusual for me to go months without a weekend. Sometimes I would plan how we were going to manage at least one day off a week, but it rarely happened.

I was burning out every year or so. I chronically underslept and overate to keep myself moving, I drank regularly to relax, I was always wired. If my chronic stress was a likely cause of cancer, then the way I dealt with that stress only exacerbated things, for sleep and food and alcohol have an effect on hormones too, and:

> *One of the chief ways that emotions act biologically in cancer causation is through the effect of hormones. Some hormones—estrogen, for example—encourage tumour growth. Others enhance cancer development by reducing the immune system's capacity to destroy malignant cells. Hormone production is intimately affected by psychological stress.*

I always wonder, if I had known this, really known how toxic stress can be to the body, would I have let it get as bad as it got? Because my work is personally rewarding and satisfying, and because I felt privileged to have it, I found it almost impossible to limit my commitments. Even when I had been diagnosed with cancer, I found it incredibly difficult to let go of work until my colleagues told me to leave it, that it wasn't my problem any more.

It is only after the physical danger has passed that I am able to analyse my own overwork compulsion at a deeper level: I am a Māori woman at the top level of her field, and what I feel about this, a lot of the time, is shame. Who am I to do well when so many do not? It takes cancer to show me my shame. It takes cancer to show me that the way I have been dealing with that shame is to work myself into the ground. It is never enough to work for myself or my family—somehow, I make the profound need for more Māori in my field my responsibility too. The shame says I am not worthy. The shame says I am not 'Māori enough', even though I tell others, constantly, that the only thing that defines us as Māori is whakapapa. I am whakamā, all the time. It is suddenly clear that this deep whakamā is one of the conditions that caused my cancer.

It was not until I was wheeled into recovery from my own cancer surgery that I saw government minister Kiri Allan's announcement that she had stage three cervical cancer. I was heartbroken and shocked for her in a way I hadn't been for myself. At stage one, my condition was barely comparable to hers. As Allan revealed in the *New Zealand Herald*, her predicted rate of survival was 13 percent because she is wahine Māori. The rate for non-Māori for the same cancer is 40 percent survival. 'The total-cancer mortality rate among Māori adults was more than 1.5 times as high as that among non-Māori adults', and at times it is much higher.

When I think about Kiri and about academic and writer, Teresia Teaiwa, who is sadly and sorely missed, as well as others who have been sick while working in high-level, high-stress environments, I wonder if I should write about the cost of success for Māori and Pasifika women, even though I can't tell anyone else's story but my own. In a session called 'Fast Burning Women' at the 2018 WORD Festival in Christchurch, Selina Tusitala Marsh and Tusiata Avia talked about how to manage the demands of success on our time and wellbeing, the strategies we must use to place limits on what others ask of us. It's a frequent conversation among Indigenous Pasifika and Māori women: how to keep success from swallowing us up with its demands on our energy and our voices. The cancers that grow in our bodies, and the other illnesses we manifest, tell us that it is a life and death conversation.

*

An Adverse Childhood Experiences (ACE) score is a diagnostic tool, and one that doesn't tell us everything, but is known to be a fairly accurate predictor of higher risk for health problems later in life: a high score means more likelihood of addiction, cancers and other diseases, and mental health disorders. My ACE score is eight out of ten if you include things I can't remember, but which I know to be true. By this or any sociological measure, I shouldn't be where I am today. Sometimes a high ACE score can be mitigated by a caring grandparent or other caregiver, but I didn't have those as a child either. It was creativity that saved me, and some sort of fierce mentality that refused to believe what I was told about life from a young age. But there's only so much you can keep at bay, and while I kept my mind intact, I seem to have absorbed a whole lot into my body. We can call this trauma, or traumatic stress or chronic stress, but it's more complex than a single label. I was relieved to escape from that childhood, though I immediately walked into a relationship that replicated those conditions, and then I became a single parent.

For a long time, I thought I could absorb it all, everything that came at us, me and my daughters. If I could just hold everything together with my mind, all the shattered pieces, and just keep everything at bay with my body—the ancestral body, the Hinenuitepō body, the thickset, fast-twitch genes body, the stressed-out, sleep-deprived, overfed body—then I could keep us safe. If I just stayed awake long enough, was hypervigilant enough, was persistent enough, strong enough, clever enough, healthy enough, good enough, present enough, available enough, both soft and hard enough, if I could just be enough, I would come between my daughters and all the hard things and all the hard people—the ones we know and the ones we don't know, the systemic violence, the lateral violence, even, sometimes the raw old-fashioned emotional and physical violence. But I was kidding myself. I didn't stop the world getting through. Heck, some of the time I was the one who brought it in.

And then, quite far into adulthood, things came right. Life got good. I started writing, seriously. I found community. I put down my weapons, disassembled my imaginary walls. Writing requires an openness and vulnerability that I wouldn't have if I was still in survival mode. But the thing about healing is, the further along you go, the better equipped you become to deal with the stuff that was left undone in childhood or even adulthood. Sometimes I believe if I can just get it together enough, I won't have to deal with it all circling back around again and again. And again. Trauma is exhausting this way: put full stops against it all you like but it will come back when it is least expected.

Maté describes how in most cases, there is a clear precursor to the onset of disease—some kind of acute stress or fracture in social relationships. Against the backdrop of all the conditions that were already primed in my life, encouraged by my own actions and those of others, the thing that tipped the scales for me was an incidence of lateral violence. Our judgements of each other can be harsher and more painful than anything the coloniser can dish out (maybe I just don't care about the coloniser's opinions). When we take each other down, for our mahi, our creativity, our intellect, or for taking a risk and amplifying our voices, we act out the worst of what colonisation has done to us. This experience is not unusual, yet we fear to talk about it openly because it detracts from the real fight. It's powerfully insidious: the wounded feel isolated, alienated and undermined.

My uncle, Sir Mason Durie, introduced Te Whare Tapa Whā in the 1980s, demonstrating the four aspects of health for Māori: tinana, wairua, hinengaro, whānau, or physical, spiritual, mental and emotional, family and social. Some models add whenua or land/roots to this structure. The whare needs all walls of the house, and its foundation, to stand. When hurtful action comes from within the marginalised community, it causes deep fracture for the marginalised psyche: it's like taking a wrecking ball to the walls of our whare tapa whā. And what we are left with is an intensification of whakamā.

*

I have two good friends in other parts of the country who have much worse cancers than me, one Māori and one Pākehā, one male and one female. They are both kind and concerned about my diagnosis, but I share it with them mainly in solidarity with their own, because connecting with them is always an exercise in helplessness and inadequacy. I feel very sure about what my cancer means to me, but when I see it in other people, it makes no sense. It seems extremely unfair. Making meaning from this disease is something that works for me. But my conviction shouldn't be mistaken for arrogance about what cancer is or why anyone else has it: I didn't think I'd ever be here, and I don't understand why my friends are.

By the time my diagnosis comes, despite everything that has preceded it, I am better off than I have ever been, and that makes it easy to see my particular diagnosis as a gift: a nudge, a quiet talking-to, a sharply focusing lens.

'It's okay,' I told my sister, when she fretted for me from overseas, 'I'm so lucky. It'd be different if I was alone.' For a long time, I was alone, or with people who were the opposite of my husband. 'Moea he tangata ringa raupā', the whakataukī says, 'marry someone with calloused hands'. The implication: they'll look after you. Somehow, eventually, I did, and he does. Being married to an emotionally healthy individual is, on the scale of things I expected to see in my life, a miracle. He is simply willing to do the work, whatever that work is, even when the work is on himself. Recovery is much harder without a crew like this.

'Reparations!' my eldest exclaims when she sees her Pākehā matua whāngai (adoptive parent) doing this work. Nothing gets past anyone in this house. It's true, his efforts are making up for transgressions that go beyond either of us. There is a clear understanding in our home that much of the damage we still carry is directly attributable to a family history that microcosmically replicates the colonial process. Colonial violence has fed into the lives of my children through both sides of their heritage. As Resmaa Menakem explains in *My Grandmother's Hands,* trauma exists in the body rather than the emotions, and is routinely passed on from person to person, generation to generation. Whatever we're dealing with has been there for a long time, and likely began long before us.

*

Frankenboob changes everything. The way I eat, the way I sleep, the way I drink. How I think, how I speak, what I give my attention to. But none of this is because of treatment or what I have been prescribed. Every practitioner I meet at the hospital is exceedingly kind, gentle, and clearly hard-working. They ask me how I am, but they mean how my body is, particularly the areas affected by treatment. I can access counselling if I wish, through the Breast Cancer Society, though access to Māori counsellors is notoriously difficult. It's been forty years since we've known about Te Whare Tapa Whā, but in several months of treatment, no one asks me about my whānau. No one asks about my wairua or hinengaro. I wouldn't even have minded if they did this the Pākehā way. They could have talked to me about my diet, coping mechanisms, exercise, support systems. I'm fine because I have good access to information, and I'm a researcher, but I think a lot about people who only do what the doctor prescribes. People who don't have the time or energy or easy access to research, people for whom English is not the first language, or who have a big family waiting for them to get home with the kai. It's the only thing that worries me— that our treatment is limited to the body parts in which the cancer has grown. And it would make a difference, to have someone ask about our lives as a whole. The evidence is clear that the way we feed and exercise and relax ourselves can make a huge difference to our outcomes. The evidence is clear that we should pray or meditate, deal with our chronic stress, make amends and decide how to respond to those who have harmed us. The evidence is clear we should forgive ourselves, most of all, and live in good community with others.

During the three weeks of radiotherapy, my breast became uncomfortable and itchy and sore. It lost some skin and received a radiation tan. But mostly it's the fatigue people talk about, and that was the hard part. Still, there's nothing quite like cancer as a legitimate excuse to not work. By the time my convalescence was over, I'd gotten used to something called rest, and I've become unwilling to forget that it means life.

I'm still figuring out how to deal with the conditions that caused the cancer. It's all of the above and then some, with some element of chaos and free radicals and the way the fucking world is right now. At my one-year check-up, I was given the all-clear—the name Frankenboob faded long ago with her scars, though there might still be a tinge of blue. The oncologist said it takes one year to recover from surgery, two to recover from radiation. I wonder how long it takes to recover from the conditions that caused the cancer. It could be generations, but there's no reason it can't start now.

REFERENCES

Women with a history … Gabor Maté, *When the Body Says No: The cost of hidden stress* (Scribe Publications, 2019), p. 73.

Research has suggested … Ibid., p. 76.

One of the chief ways … Ibid., p. 75.

her predicted rate of survival … 'Kiri Allan reveals grim cancer prognosis', *New Zealand Herald*, 4 May 2021.

The total-cancer mortality … 'Cancer', Manatū Hauora–Ministry of Health, 2 August 2018: www.health. govt.nz/search/results/total%20cancer%20rate

incidence of lateral violence … 'Lateral violence is displaced violence; that is, anger and rage directed towards members within a marginalised or oppressed community by their peers rather than towards the oppressors of the community', Geraldine Moane, *Gender and colonialism: A psychological analysis of oppression and liberation* (Palgrave Macmillan, 2011).

trauma exists in the body … Resmaa Menakem, *My Grandmother's Hands: Racialized trauma and the pathway to mending our hearts and bodies* (Central Recovery Press, 2017).

TĪHEMA BAKER

Whakapapa

It wasn't the first grave I'd dug. But it was the first time I'd found somebody already in one.

The grave was for my grand-aunty—my koro's sister, the latest of his siblings to pass. Dad, as he always did, dropped everything to offer what support he could to the whānau pani. So did his siblings, like my aunties, who came down from Taranaki and installed themselves in the kitchen. It was automatic, an unspoken, shared understanding that they'd gone through this with Koro, so now it was their turn to support their cousins in the loss of their mother.

But something seemed different this time. Rather seamlessly, Dad assumed control of the entire event, not in a commanding way but as a gentle, guiding force for the rest of the whānau to follow.

I wondered if this was partly due to what I'd said a few months earlier at my wedding, when I asked Dad to bless our kai. I explained to our guests that once we would have asked Koro to do this for us as our kaumātua. With his passing, that mana now rested with Dad, a koro himself. I expected him to step up into this role for our whānau.

The way he took charge of this tangi was the first time since that night that I felt like he'd heard me. Watching him in action, I realised I should help too. It was a small tangi, and most jobs were filled already. The kitchen was full of cooks under the command of my aunties, and a diligent squad of rangatahi seemed to have the packing up and down of the wharekai between meals under control. Looking around the wharenui, there appeared to be a shortage of young tāne to help with a job like digging the grave. I decided that would be my contribution, so I reported to Dad for duty, and he agreed to assign me, along with three of my cousins, as grave diggers.

My grand-aunty was to be buried at Mutikotiko, the hill at our urupā behind Rangiātea Church in Ōtaki. There is land on this hill reserved for my whānau. Years earlier, it was there that I dug a grave for the first time under the instruction of Dad and joined by my tuakana and cousin-in-law. That grave was for my grand-uncle—another of Koro's siblings—and, being my first time, I learned there was far more to grave-digging than I thought. There is a skill to it, technical details you need to remember, like forming a little pillow out of dirt for the head of the coffin, which creates space under the rest of it so that the ropes used to lower it into the grave can be pulled back out again. You have to know the soil and how to work it, which we discovered the hard way when the entire left wall collapsed under my brother's gumboots. The soil of Mutikotiko is almost like sand, which makes for easy digging, but fragile holes. We'd failed to protect the soft edges of the grave with planks of wood, which we paid for when my brother walked along one of them.

It's comical now, that image of him: sprawled out on a cascade of sand, halfway in the grave, barely holding himself up with a shovel wedged desperately into the top corner. At the time, it was anything but funny; there was a silent, unequivocal look of 'Oh fuck' that flitted between each of us before we leapt into action, hauling him out of the grave and frantically trying to work out how to fix the now half-refilled hole before everyone arrived. That was grave-digging lesson number one: it's harder than it looks.

Beyond the physical challenge of it, though, lies the spiritual. By digging into the earth of an urupā, you are exposing yourself to one of the most powerful types of tapu; the tapu of death. It permeates everything, including the soil. But on Mutikotiko, I learned, you're just as likely to encounter the direct source of that tapu—the dead that lie within it. The hill, Dad informed us, is filled with unmarked graves and coming across kōiwi is a distinct possibility. In fact, they'd found some when digging the grave for another grand-aunty, which happened to be right next to the one we were digging then for her brother.

I asked Dad what they did when they found the kōiwi.

'We put it aside, said a little karakia, then put it back when we were finished.'

He made it sound so simple—nothing to be afraid of.

But I was struck by an uncomfortable sense of anticipation. A morbid curiosity at the prospect of uncovering real human remains evoked an intensely spiritual fear of the same. The tapu of death had always unnerved me beyond what could be considered an ordinary respectful regard for it. I put this down to an experience in my childhood where, at another tangi in Kuku north of Ōtaki, I removed a child's shoes that were sitting on top of a grave. In my naivety, I thought someone had left them behind. When I showed Dad, thinking he would know how to find their owner, he erupted with anger. He dragged me by the arm back to the urupā, where he commanded me to return the shoes and uttered a karakia to make amends for what I had done. Afterwards, once the misdeed had been corrected and his anger had subsided, he explained to me why he had reacted that way and how I had exposed myself to the tapu of death in a way that wasn't safe. It felt like that moment in *The Lion King* where, after rescuing Simba from the hyenas, Mufasa says he was only angry at Simba because he was afraid. I didn't want to know what could frighten a man like my dad.

In the end, no kōiwi showed up in that first grave-digging experience. With its edges thoroughly planked, the hastily redug hole survived the gathering of whānau around it, the pallbearers bracing against its edges as they lowered the casket, and the mourners walking alongside it to drop soil in. Once we'd finished filling in the hole, we diggers went to the pub—a contemporary take on the tikanga that diggers don't eat at the hākari with everyone else due to the residual tapu on them.

All these memories—these learnings—were with me as Dad dropped me off at the urupā on the cold, rainy morning of my grand-aunty's burial. My three cousins and I were to be directed in the digging by Uncle Mark, who was, by all accounts, 'the man' at digging graves. I felt more prepared this time, more certain of what to expect—which, because my cousins had never dug a grave before, made me somehow the most experienced behind Uncle Mark. I knew that the coffin-shaped frame we'd brought with us up the hill would give us the size we needed to adhere to; I knew that we would begin by marking the outline with our shovels first and removing the top grassy layer in squares; I knew that the most efficient way to dig would be to take turns, each of us digging out a layer from one end to the other while the others either rested or helped keep the growing mound of dug-out soil nice and tidy. I also knew what Uncle Mark informed my cousins before we began: that we might come across kōiwi.

What I didn't know was how it would actually feel when we did. It was my turn to dig a layer, and that sandy soil, despite being thickened by the constant rain, made it easy to lose myself in the rhythm of the work; the shunt of the shovel's blade into the soil, the brace of my legs as I lifted out a clump, the swing of dirt up over the grave's edge, the flick of the handle to dump the load. Over and over, muscles burning, back aching. Shunt, brace, lift, swing, flick. Until my shovel hit something harder than soil and the whole cycle came to a jarring halt.

It couldn't have been more like that classic Hollywood scene: the ominous thud, the pause, the moment of realisation. I withdrew the shovel, scraped aside some of the dirt until I felt it again—a shape in the earth.

'You found something?'

My cousins, leaning on their shovels and chatting away on a well-earned break, hadn't noticed. But Uncle Mark had been watching the whole time.

I cleared away more dirt, revealing two long shapes that could have been nothing more than a pair of sticks. Uncle Mark and I both knew they weren't.

'Hand them up.'

I did as I was told. Bent down and retrieved the kōiwi. In the moment, I thought nothing profound about the fact that I was holding the bones of another human being in my bare hand. But later, I would reflect on the way I proffered them up to Uncle Mark with both hands and the near-identical way he received them, placing them gently, reverently, beside the grave.

Then it was back to work. Like we hadn't just made an archaeological discovery. Like we hadn't just disturbed someone's final resting place. I settled back into the rhythm of digging until I had completed my layer, at which point Uncle Mark ordered me out of the hole. We swapped places, and while he took to shearing down the walls of the grave with his spade, I began to fill my cousins in on what I'd found.

That was when we heard the second thud.

Uncle Mark wasn't, as I'd assumed, just straightening the grave's walls. He was checking for more kōiwi. And, as my cousins and I discovered while leaning over the grave to watch him work, that's exactly what he'd found.

An ivory-coloured dome was protruding from the sheer wall of the grave, right near where I'd found the other bones. A human skull. Just sticking out of the earth like that.

We watched Uncle Mark delicately excavate the dirt around it until it rolled onto the floor of the grave. He picked it up and looked at us.

'Someone take this.'

I didn't move. The skull personified these remains in a way that the other bones hadn't. Something in me drew a line at touching this person's head. At holding a human skull in my hands. And something else, a part of me I had almost forgotten—a little boy who took a pair of shoes from an urupā— suddenly, powerfully, wished my dad was there.

My paralytic reaction went unnoticed; one of my cousins promptly stepped forward and took the skull from Uncle Mark. I can still see that image—the stark colour of the cranium against the grey and brown drudgery of the day, the way the bottom jaw unexpectedly flopped open and my cousin fumbled to keep it together. He placed it with the other bones beside the grave, where it became the centrepiece of a growing pile of kōiwi that we continued to unearth.

Every time I finished my layer and hauled myself out of the grave, my eyes were drawn to that pile. I couldn't stop thinking about who this person was— were they a man or a woman? Elderly or in the prime of their adulthood? There was every chance they could have been my direct tūpuna. I'd never know.

Maybe Dad somehow sensed that cosmic cry for his presence because he eventually appeared to check in on our progress—probably one of the many rounds he was doing that morning. He caught my eye, and I directed his gaze to the kōiwi. He let out a small sigh, then said to my cousins and me, 'Everybody feel all good about that?'

I wasn't sure exactly how I felt about it. I certainly felt *something*. It was just hard to pinpoint what it was. All I knew was that uncovering and handling these kōiwi had placed me in an extreme state of tapu. Perhaps that was the feeling seeping through me—something indefinable, a power beyond comprehension. To answer Dad's question, it wasn't a bad feeling. Just one I'd never felt before.

So, copying my cousins, I gave a stoic grunt in the affirmative, and Dad left us to it. The work continued under Uncle Mark's direction, who cemented his 'the-man-at-digging-graves' status by screwing together a frame made from two sheets of wood and four posts, which we slid into the grave to brace the walls once they started showing signs of fragility. It was an ingenious invention, crafted to pinpoint precision, which I couldn't stop thinking was sorely needed at that first grave I'd dug with my brother and cousin-in-law.

We stopped once we came across a second set of kōiwi at the opposite end of the grave. It wasn't as deep as it probably should have been—only about five feet—but Uncle Mark said that was far enough. He crafted the little 'pillow' for the head of the coffin and dug an extra square into the floor of the grave. That was where the kōiwi, which we carefully passed down to him, were reinterred. Then the small hole was filled and levelled off, and none of the mourners who brought my grand-aunty up to Mutikotiko later would know it had ever been there.

The rest of the day passed in a relative haze. I spent the afternoon mostly processing what I'd learned, reflecting on it all. Uncle Mark, my cousins, and I waited out the church service in a small shed with a box of Export Golds that Dad left us. Then, after the service was complete, we filled the grave back in, said our final karakia, washed the muck from all our gear, and downed the rest of our beers.

Before he left, Uncle Mark told me he'd been looking for someone to replace him.

'I'm getting too old for this,' he said with a chuckle. 'Think it's time for another generation to step up.'

I laughed it off; I didn't feel ready to be responsible for something like that and wasn't entirely sure that 'gravedigger' was the type of role I wanted to fill within our whānau, hapū and iwi when it came to tangihanga.

When Dad picked me up these thoughts were still swimming in my head. He asked me again if I felt okay about it all, and I told him that I did—but that a part of me wondered if I *shouldn't* feel okay. I could still feel the weight of that tapu on me. Despite having said our karakia and cleansed ourselves with water from the urupā tap, I didn't feel totally clean—physically or spiritually. I wanted a hot shower to wash all the earth from me and some space to process everything.

Dad assured me that there was nothing to worry about. He said we'd been cautious and respectful in our treatment of those kōiwi.

'At the end of the day, son,' he concluded, 'they're our tūpuna. Who better to care for them than us?'

It seemed then that Dad had become a kaumātua in his own right. Someone to look to; for guidance, for counsel, for wisdom. I wasn't the only one he had given this feeling of assurance and safety throughout the tangi. He'd done this for everyone. Not because he wanted to, but because there was no one else. His father's generation—my Koro's—was almost gone; we'd just buried another of them. So he'd heard the call. His time had come to step up.

And so, I realised, had mine.

Reasons to Learn Cantonese

1

My grandfather gave me my name at birth:文麗 | Mun4 Lai6. The first character, a family name, means *the arts*; the second means *beautiful*. Years later, when we lived in the same city, he made me practise the characters in long columns to get the strokes just right, this stern old man whose every smile had to be earned. 公公 | Gung1 Gung1 was himself a master calligrapher: he had the traditional ink and brushes, which I was not allowed to touch, and had painted placards all around the house.

When I was asked as a child what my middle name was, I gave the German middle name my parents had chosen, Elisabeth, which already seemed unusual enough for its spelling. I pretended often to have no other middle name. Now, I consider the love promised in naming a child and the hurt of rejecting such a gift.

2

When I studied German, I copied out page after page of irregular verbs until I knew the whole song: *befehlen, befahl, befohlen; gelingt, gelang, gelungen*. It took me a whole year to learn all of them, from *backen* to *zwingen*, but it's a finite list; the same every time I google 'irregular German verbs'. Mastering it, I immediately began to sound less like a foreigner.

Tense construction in Cantonese is simpler, relying on context or a single modifier. You do not have to say *I went to the airport*, you can say *I go to the airport yesterday*. There are no irregular verbs. There is also no separate plural form for most nouns, and only one pronoun for *he* and *she*. On the other hand, I can't guess a single new word, because nothing looks like English. On the other hand, there is no alphabet, only many thousands of distinct characters. On the other hand, the language uses a complex system of units whenever a noun is presented with a quantity. *One apple*, 一个苹果 | yat1 go3 ping4 gwo2, means something like *one of the apple*—only the unit, *of the*, changes depending on the noun. *Apple* and *orange* use the unit for small, round things. *Cucumber* and *whole fish* use the unit for long, thin things. This seems intuitive until I learn that *hour* and *person* and *television* also use the unit for small, round things. There is no finite list of verbs I can memorise, and I am still trying to figure out how I can make myself sound less like a foreigner.

3

There are so many words I already know. At least one appears in each class, waving at me from a mass of unintelligible others, like a small friend. 快啲 | Faai3 di1 laa1 (*hurry up*), 垃圾 | laap6 saap3 (*rubbish*), 洗手 | sai2 sau2 (*wash your hands*), 瞓覺 | faan3 gau3 (*sleeping*). For almost two years of my childhood, we lived in my grandparents' house, where rice was eaten with every dinner and the placards on the wall promised 长寿 (*longevity*) and 和平 (*peace*). Under the erosions of my white schooling, I did not think I had kept so much.

4

Cantonese contains at least six tones: the same word, said with minutely different inflections, can mean *four* or *dead*. Something about this reminds me of wordless nature: the language of birds wheeling over the lake, or the dim that comes over the earth during an eclipse. I did not think there was a language closer to those things than English, in which I can write anything I like. But it turns out writing is the opposite of a certain kind of knowledge.

5

While we don't learn to write or read the characters, they are printed on our handouts. I'm amazed at how close some of the words look to what they mean; at what seems, to an English speaker, like the collapse of signifier and signified: 狗 (*dog*); 人 (*person*); 木 (*tree*); 雨 (*rain*). The word *rain* in English is so familiar to me it's almost invisible, but beneath the surface teem a host of unconscious associations: echoes of the words *ray* and *pain* and *reign* and *rein*; a certain openness implied by the vowel. In Cantonese, the homonyms of 雨 | jyu5 include 宇 | jyu5 (*space),* 語 | jyu5 (*language),* and 羽 | jyu5 (*feather*). I am only beginning to imagine a world in which *rain* is unconsciously associated with *feathers*.

6

When the war come, the first son, he swim to Hong Kong, the second son, he ...
She does not have the English to finish. But I would like to know what happened
to the second son, and the third, and their mother.

7

Every few weeks, I video call my friend Willa, who speaks Cantonese fluently.
With her, I practise the names of fruits I have learnt—苹果 | ping4 gwo2 (*apple*),
橙 | chaang2 (*orange*), 西瓜 | saai1 gwaa1 (*watermelon*). *What about pomelos?*
she asks. I tell her we didn't learn the word for pomelo and she looks appalled.
But it's an important fruit! she says, which makes me so fond of her I feel like
crying. I met Willa when she was doing a Law master's degree in English, her
fourth language. Once, she asked me to check an essay for her, where not one
word was out of place. Now she teaches me the word 柚 | jau2 (*pomelo*) with
such patience, I'm reminded language exists only to bridge two people.

8

One year, in London, my flatmate's extended family came around for Christmas
lunch. I came downstairs to say hello. *Oh*, said her mother to me, *are you the
children's nanny? No no, this is my flatmate*, said my flatmate. *Oh, but I thought*,
said her mother, but she did not finish her thought, which hung understood in
the air. Nobody apologised. I left the room. *It might not have been racial*, said my
white boyfriend later.

9

My father is a white man. Once, when we are out for lunch together, the waiter
hesitates for a second, then says to him *and what will your wife have?* and I
remember again, as I do every time we are together, that I do not look like him.
I will always be unlike my father, which is a kind of grief. Part of me wishes I
could be only white. Another part is furious I could ever have such a wish.

10

There are so many questions I cannot ask in English: *What was the trip like?*
Were you frightened? How did people treat you when you arrived? What is the

worst thing a New Zealander has ever said to you? Do you ever regret coming here? What lives did you hope for, for your children? Do you think they got them? Will you give my children Chinese names, even if they do not look Chinese? Are you lonely?

11

Why are you learning Cantonese? I am asked almost every time I mention it. *What made you start now? Where exactly,* says someone leaning in to parse my face, *are you from?* I am a walking question, one that strangers stop to ask. But I still don't know the answer. What does it mean to be half-Chinese? How do you carry the genes of both a group that is regularly discriminated against and a group that regularly discriminates in one body? Who are you in the eyes of the world and who are you quietly, within yourself? I am the custodian of a body that could never pass for white. More than anything, I would like to know myself.

12

I wanted to write about learning German. I learned German because I loved the serpentine grammar, because I romanticise Bach, and because I wanted, once, to be other than myself. I worked at it until I mastered it, and all my work was joy.

Learning Cantonese is about guilt and obligation and wist. I am slow and I do not love it, partly because it does not feel quite like my choice. In its thickets, I cannot pretend to be other than myself. I do not think I will ever master it.

13

I don't study as much as I should between classes, although I think about the fact I cannot speak it every single day.

RACHEL BUCHANAN

The Cares

You can't hug someone on Zoom. You can watch them cry, though. You can watch them try and lift their hands to their face to dry their tears. You can see their nose is dripping. You know they are distressed because they want to blow their nose and wipe their eyes, but they cannot remember how to do these things. There is no hanky or tissue.

You say: 'Mum, Mum. Mary. It's alright.' You can see carers walking behind your mother, carrying plates of food for other residents. The tears keep falling. You reach through the screen and dry your mother's face, hold her hand, kiss her cheek. You are Tom Cruise. This is *Minority Report*. You can rearrange the future. Or the past. Time is immaterial. You are a man and you drive a miniature helicopter and you have an arsenal of military-grade killing apparatus strapped to your body. You imagine smashing the computer screen and smashing the kitchen table and smashing your cup of herbal tea. You imagine drinking any amount of alcohol, cocktails and IPA beers, a bottle of sparkling Shiraz. Te Ao Moemoea, baby. Those dreams could come true, quite easily. You call the nursing home. Press 2 for the hospital wing. Hold music. When a voice answers, you hang up. Distress, fizzy drink bursting from the bottle. You call Aditi, one of the carers. You send a text message. And another. Please, Aditi, can someone help Mary blow her nose?

Your mother is wearing a beanie and pink headphones. The headphones are crooked. She is a cosmic DJ. She is on a bender. She is getting the party started. You tell your mother it is alright. 'Hang on, Mum,' you say. You look at her wet face and runny nose and think, love, love, love. What a pretty spell. It doesn't work. All you feel is fury. It's 2.20pm in Melbourne, 4.20pm in Wellington on one of the 112 days of Melbourne's second lockdown. What is a day? A day is an obstacle between you and your bed and the iPad. Covid-19 coronavirus pandemic circuit breaker mega lockdown staying apart keeps us together. The trains still run. They carry no one, nowhere. In your dreams, a throng. Touching, breathing, hugging, kissing, like church in the 1970s in New Plymouth. Guitars play. A tambourine. In the basement, Sara and her family speak in tongues. So much hair.

You sit at your kitchen table in Melbourne. In your lap, the dress that caused the tears. Your mother made it for you when you were thirteen. It is lilac georgette. You and your mother bought the fabric from Ward's on Devon Street, New Plymouth. It was really expensive. You can't remember how much now. You also bought a white lace collar for the dress, a belt buckle and stiffening to make a belt for the dress and a Vogue designer pattern. Rating: très difficile. The dress had dozens of pintucks. The tucks were all different lengths but designed to form an upside-down starburst across the bodice and below the waist. Pin cushion, measuring tape, the rata-tata-tat of the needle. You recall your mother pinning the fabric, the hours it took to get it right, the crinkle of the pattern tissue, the sound of the scissors against the gold wood of the kitchen table. It was kauri, an old shop counter, a canvas for the artist. Your mother. Pregnant with kid number eight. A total embarrassment. Don't your parents have a telly? Catholics breed like rabbits. Babies are pests.

The dress was too old for you. Or too young. A Peter Pan lace collar. A novitiate. Black suede peep-toe shoes made by Andrea Biani. Long curly hair, a thin purple ribbon as an Alice band. Demure and delicate in the era of punk. Third form, fourth form, one of those years, a formal at Gladstones Dance Academy, Blagdon. Sacred Heart Girls College and Francis Douglas Boys College united for one night. No one asked you to dance. Wallflower. You hid in the loos, stood on the sidelines, hated yourself and your bad skin, watched the other kids kiss.

Your mother kept the dress. New Plymouth, Masterton, Hamilton, Wellington, the dress moved with her. You moved away. Masterton, Wellington, Queenstown, Invercargill, Hamilton, Piedmont mountains, Newcastle Upon Tyne, Scottish Highlands, London, Melbourne. How had the dress survived? Why had your mother given it back to you? Not exactly a scene of triumph. Your daughters had tried it on. Oh, the beauty. But none of them wanted to wear it. The dress belonged not just to a different era but a different dimension. Glass display case. Interactive 3D information panel. Soundscape. Yet today, you got it out of the cupboard and decided to use it as a prop in the weekly Zoom. An endurance event. Your mother locked in a nursing home in Wellington; you locked in your home in Melbourne. One week Aditi was wearing a white mask with a big yellow smiley mouth on it. Jack Nicholson, *The Joker*. Seven months of calls. Every Thursday, the encounter.

Photos, poems, Bible, uke, dress. *Because the Lord is My Shepherd I have everything I need!* Your mother is wearing a beanie and pink headphones. She is a fortune teller. She stares into her crystal ball. A lilac dress emerges from the depths. A voice comes with it. The voice says thank you. The voice conjures up the sound of the scissors on the kitchen table, how hard it was to get the pintucks right, the challenge of making the belt and getting the lace collar to sit right. The voice mentions the lace borders on each sleeve and says they are pretty. The voice says the dress is pretty. It is exquisite. You hold the dress in your hands, the fine, sheer, pale fabric, the thin belt, the purple buttons. It's not you. It never was. That's not what this is about.

You look at the screen and thank your mother for giving you your life, for loving you, for all the beautiful things she made for you (the dress, the reversible tweed bomber jacket like the one Princess Di wore in her engagement photo, the grey wool dropped-waist dress with box pleats, the blue and black checked pinafore, the acid-washed brown denim jumpsuit, the pale blue blazer with white buttons, the black velvet bodycon ball dress). You thank her for driving you to ballet lessons and classical guitar lessons and rehearsals, for encouraging you to do Little Rep, play cricket, basketball, netball and soccer, for coming on the train—with a toddler, your baby brother—from Masterton to Wellington to attend your graduation from Wellington Polytechnic. You had earned a Diploma in Journalism. Average mark, a solid C. Later, for asking you about your writing. The creation of this dress—and the keeping of this dress—is evidence of your mother's love. The long-ago school dance, the crying in the loos, those old feelings of shame and rejection at being left alone on the sidelines, all of that is overridden by this sudden insight. You hold the dress in your lap. Your mother was the one who asked you to dance!

For the first time, it feels easy to keep the pledge you have made, the promise to only say good things, kind things, to your mother on Zoom. You don't mention the hurts. There are some. Fake it till you make it, but now you are actually telling the truth. It's unbelievable! 'Thank you so much, Mum.' Your mother starts to cry. You can't hug someone on Zoom. You text Aditi. You hold the dress.

*

The aim was to touch her again. That's what you wanted. Hug, kiss, hold hands. In mid-2020, the travel bubble would come up, sometimes, on the news. 'Mum! The bubble!' your daughters would shout. Jacinda was about to say yes. Then, more cases. So no. Pop. Pop. Pop. Six months' leave from work, most of it supposed to be spent in Aotearoa New Zealand, researching and writing and being with Mum. That was clearly not going to happen. Extend the leave; keep hoping. Nup. Then it was 2021. You had to stop the Zooms. Too painful. Your big baby, stuck in her La-Z-Boy, glaring at you, chewing her lips. Above, a bouffant of grey hair. Behind, a watercolour by Joanna Paul. *For Mary. A greenness at the centre.* In drawers, cupboards and baskets, many sets of rosary beads. All tremendously cheap and ugly. Where the hell had they come from? *You're my mother now.*

The last time you saw Mum in real life was 12 March 2020. By then, the air had started to change. It wasn't innocent any more. The air was a topic to consider. Like high-touch surfaces. And people who coughed and sneezed in public. And the dangers of being in lifts, buses, trains, airports, escalators, hotels, shops, public toilets. The cruise ship was a gargantuan supermarket pav. Floating petrie dish. Not your line. The cable car disgorged dozens of elderly tourists, mostly American, into the Botanical Gardens and surrounds. Even their camera bags seemed sinister. Incubators. Asymptomatic. Autoclave. Superspreaders. The words popped up from nowhere. They should go home. You should go home. Would the flight still run?

Go hard and go early, as Jacinda would soon say.

On 13 March 2020, you were the only person on board who was not off to the Grand Prix. By the time the plane touched down in Melbourne, the event had been called off, and there was no toilet paper in the shops. Your family was unprepared. You had to grovel to get loo paper, find friends with a stash and beg. On Instagram, women posted photos of masks. Black, checked or vintage. It was an irritating but novel situation. Netflix was there to help. And SBS On Demand. *The Spiral. The Bureau. The Crown. The Last Dance.* That stupid film about the South African man who fell in love with the octopus. And *Dick Johnson is Dead*, Kirsten Johnson's masterpiece starring her dad and his Alzheimer's and various stuntmen. Instruction manual. If you can't handle tragedy, choose comedy.

Back then, in March, Mary could still talk. She could stand and sit on her own. She could walk, feed herself, go to the loo on her own (more or less), wash her hands (again, assistance required), brush her hair, potter, whistle, sing, dance, remember all the words to say at Mass and read, or at least fake read, in a pretty convincing fashion. A small red *Daily Missal. Communio* magazines. Letters and cards, a Legion of Mary pamphlet or two.

By the end of 2020, few of these skills remained.

Mum could still whistle. You'd whistled together on Zoom. She could still laugh and cry, make monster noises. Mum could still place a few words together, side by side, in order. *That's lovely. Oh yes. I do. Of course, I know who that is. Mum! Leo. We ate our dinners there.* She could listen and respond to passages from the Bible, to poems, to funny little jokes. 'Hi Mum. This is Rachel. I am your first-born child and also your favourite. Total number one!' That cracked her up every time.

Her memory had been clear-felled. There were no more stories about picking peas, riding bareback or driving the Bedford truck. The holidays at Sunnyside were gone. A forest had once flourished; now, there was not even leaf cover. Just earth. Waiting for the sun or the rain or even a cup of tea. A smile. A familiar outline. A voice that might breeze through the understorey, stirring something up, ruffling the leaf-shaped spaces inside her brain. *You are my lovely …*

Mum lived in the over-heated now, the never-ending now, the modest bubble of now, the super Zen chill eternal universe of now. She wore comfortable clothes, stayed hydrated, breathed. Her life was like one big yoga retreat, with a special focus on seated poses. She was as vulnerable as it is possible to be. Other people showered her, dressed her, brushed her hair, clipped her nails. This process was called 'the cares'.

When you take away the accessories, what is left? A woman with a name and a photograph on the door of her room. A personality expressed by an ongoing eagerness to eat. Her beautiful hands. Her voice. It was once very beautiful too. Elocution. Proper utterance. Fluent and elegant speaking.

Mary had spent all her life caring for other people, a mother is a word for it, and now this woman could not even care for herself. The change interested you. She was the oldest of twelve children. She was the mother of eight. She was the foster mother of two. She was the wife of one. That one took a bit of effort. Perhaps the dementia was a welcome break from it all. Mummy! Maaaaaummy. Mum! Muuuum. Mumsie. Recently, the word Mama had appeared. Women willingly called themselves that. A trend. Why? It reminded you of sheep.

When you visited, if you could visit, you wanted to hug your mother. Of course, you had other wishes too. You hoped to blow on the embers of self that were left and coax a flame that would burst into light and recognition. 'Rachel!' Mary had said your name twice in the seven months of Zoom and you hoped for more. Your name on her lips, the ultimate buzz.

'Does your mother know who you are?'

You disliked that question and had a variety of answers up your sleeve.

1. Ha, ha! No. But did she ever?
2. Yes, of course, on some deep level. Hippocampus, emotional intelligence, massage, friendliness, kindness. Rainbows. Mist. Fog. Ephemeral wetlands. Pilot light. Sunlight on the bottom of a swimming pool. Lunar eclipse. Hooray for Casey! (Casey was the nickname for an unreliable old red tractor on the family farm in Dipton. When it worked, everyone said 'hooray').
3. Wrong question. Think of another one. Is a mother's worth measured only by her ability to recognise her child? If she can no longer even recognise her child, is she still a mother? Does she even exist? Why would you want to spend time with someone who isn't even there?

Number one always got a laugh, even though it wasn't a joke. Number two was a feel-good answer. Most people liked it and so did you. Number three was a bit mean. You didn't ever say it out loud. You held back. Not everyone did.

'They should just take them out the back and shoot them.' Remark collected at Lake Ferry Hotel, October 2017. Remark made by a man whose father had dementia, after you told him your mother had dementia. Old sheepdogs, lame, mangy or mad. No use. Shotgun. Out of their misery. It was one approach, sure. Definitely save a bit of money on nursing home fees etc. It was election night. Your dad had died five days earlier. Your mum's little brother, Bill, was the incumbent. He won the most votes. Or did very well. Or should have won. Natural justice. Mists of time. But Winston Peters went with Jacinda, and Wiremu Pākehā was put out to pasture.

It was the casual confidence with which the man uttered his remark; that's what had made it stick. Like he was really sure you would agree and may even want to discuss logistics with him, weaponry and locations, numbers and paperwork. Or maybe he just wanted to make you laugh.

*

When it was clear that coronavirus was not just a bad thing that would happen to people overseas but an actual disaster in your home, your suburb, your city, you hunted for role models and inspiration. Your tūpuna from Taranaki, they were tough. They survived not just days of darkness but decades of it. One day. Just get through one day. Then the next.

Your mother could be a role model too. Your mother was tough too. You tried to imagine how your mother felt when she was diagnosed with Alzheimer's more than a decade ago. She was sixty-five, the disaster was approaching. There was nothing she could do to stop it. She pounded the table with two fists. Prayed. Certainly, there would have been a substantial amount of prayer. Hail Marys. Our Fathers. Lamb of Gods. And more complicated ones. She was fit and strong. At active seniors circuit class, the trainers called her Muscles. She had been a woman who buzzed about, ran for the bus, lugged multiple shopping bags up hills. She invented whole foods. Soybean patties, they were her signature dish. She used to make you omelettes, pick a sprig of parsley from the garden for garnish. Very little alcohol. Very little meat. Never smoked. Crosswords, jigsaw puzzles, fish, high-intensity interval training, nothing could hold back the tide. Your mother was on a beach, a very flat beach. No hills. No trees. No houses. No church steeples. The tsunami warning had been issued, and she could only wait on the flat until the big wave arrived. All memory washed away but the human remains. Maybe dementia was like menopause. Not something you can fight. Better to let yourself be carried out on the tide. Flop. Float. Seaweed. Kelp forests, barnacles, killer whales, sharks.

*

When you watched the news, you often thought about your mother. Small figure, alone on a beach. Brave and patient. The tsunami. No way to stop it. Nothing to do. No barrier between you and it. Most things out of your control. Plans smashed. School smashed. Work smashed. Holidays smashed. Concerts smashed. Parties smashed. Children, suffering. Husband, suffering. You, suffering. A mask in every pocket, dog poo on the lawn, the numbers, the pressers. Every day an obstacle. At least you had writing. Writing was your prayer. You went hard. Every day, there you were, back in Taranaki, with your tūpuna, listening to the records.

Deep clean. Abundance of caution. Click and collect. Flatten the curve. Elimination. Double donut day. The new normal. Building back better.

In April 2021, the travel bubble was inflated between Australia and New Zealand. You were cautious. You waited. You had a new job. Things were busy at work. Then you couldn't stand it and booked tickets—for you and your husband—for five days in Wellington. You had it all planned out. You would say your goodbyes to your mother. A comprehensive programme of events was planned, culminating in a trip to St Mary of the Angels on Sunday afternoon for the annual fundraising concert. A mobility taxi was ordered. Monday came. People were in a huddle at work. Four new cases of Covid-19 in Melbourne. Two days later, the bubble was paused. The trip was off. You were so upset that you went down to the swamp and started kicking fence posts. Then, you actually flung yourself sideways onto the overgrown grass and thrashed about a bit, like a dog. Your husband watched the tantrum, solemn on the outside.

*

You asked the taxi to take you straight to the nursing home. No one knew you were coming. You just woke up on Saturday morning—10 July 2021—and a voice said: Fly to Wellington on Wednesday. The day after you touched down, the bubble paused again. More cases. Melbourne would soon be in lockdown number five. You recognised the woman in reception. She was a lovely person; they all were. New Zealand, India, Ethiopia, Philippines, Mauritius, Samoa, Scotland, Australia, the carers came from all over the world. While they looked after your mother, their own mothers and fathers and grandparents and aunties and uncles and cousins struggled to stay safe and healthy in countries where there was civil war, uncontrolled coronavirus outbreaks, constitutional crisis.

'Rachel! How did you get here? Oh I am sorry. I don't think you can go in. We've just been told that we can't let anyone in from Australia. I'll check.'

The words gushed over you. You felt yourself relax. You floated, soft and empty. You realised that whatever the answer was, yes or no, you would accept it without fuss. You were truly broken. That was the word that arose from the water. Shouting and pleading would not change a thing. Covid-19 negative test, $150. One shot of AstraZeneca. The leave from work. The waiting. The anguish. The cost. The time away. You even managed to smile. The person you once were was gone, washed away by the lockdowns in Melbourne. It was alright to see her go. Now you were much more like your mother and the other brave people who lived in those rooms off the corridors. You were more like the carers, accepting and unsurprised. Everyone standing together on the beach. Without words, without memories, without footsteps, without continence, without cutlery, without visitors, without shouting, without choice, without mothers, without fathers, without God, we humans remain.

I dedicate this essay in loving memory of Mary Felicity Buchanan. Mary was born on 20 February 1945 and passed away on 24 December 2022.

JAYNE COSTELLOE

Alchemy of the Airwaves

We were station kids, my sister, brother and I. We lived on a radio station.

Not the 'What radio station are you listening to?' kind of radio station. Our radio station was a geographical location, a spot on the actual map. It was, as all radio stations were, a remote and lofty community, home to a collection of wives and children who followed the husband's job from radio station to radio station, setting up home until it was time to move on to the next radio station.

Radio stations were a phenomenon of New Zealand life in the mid-twentieth century, in the times when—other than a telephone plugged into the wall—radio was the only means of electronic communication. Radio was a vital industry, with just a tinge of glamour, and it required a national infrastructure to ensure it worked twenty-four hours a day. Stations were strung along the length and breadth of the country, from Southland to the Far North, from Murihiku to Te Tai Tokerau.

Station sites were chosen strategically, probably by a wartime cabinet, for their remoteness and isolation, for their distance and disconnection from any flotsam of civilisation tainting the surrounding landscape. Sites were chosen too for their elevation. Each radio mast looked like a poor colonial relation of the Eiffel Tower. Plain and imposing in their own way, these tall steel masts caught the radio waves flitting through the air like butterflies in a net, then flung them onwards to the next lone mast arising from the next radio station further up or further down the country.

The mast would reap the invisible net of words, then zip them down to the heart of each radio station operation—the transmitter station—purpose-built below. Here, the airwaves and airwords would be captured in huge, marbled-steel cabinets called transmitters, lined up like rows and rows of gigantic fridges, the ancestors of today's computers.

At least, I think it that's how worked. Dad knew how it worked. It was his job to know. He was a Radio Technician.

The transmitter building was always a solid concrete bunker. It was war-proof. It had to be. It was the place of work for the husbands and the dads, and it was the centre of our radio station world. Apart from the tea-room, with its incomprehensible wallpaper of naked women, the transmitter station was just one huge warm room that hummed and zinged all day and all night. It was the men's job to keep it humming and zinging so that people could keep listening to their radios. It was an important job because if there was a national emergency, like a giant tsunami or a volcanic eruption or a Viet Cong invasion, then radio was the only way to let people know what was happening.

The giant transmitter room perpetually throbbed with its wide lanes of purring transmitters. The lino was clean and soft, like a shiny carpet of cork, ideal for indoor roller-skating. Outside, the entranceway was graced by a wide sweep of concrete steps leading up into a narrow lobby, where the families' mailboxes were ranged alphabetically in cubbyholes along two walls, ready to receive our Christmas cards and their gorgeous glittering stamps.

To enter the transmitter room, you would need to heave open the thick glass-and-brass double doors from the lobby. Then you would emerge into another world, absorbed immediately into the soft, padded interior of a spaceship, engulfed by a hum and a rush of warmth. Then came the smell, polished lino mixed with a uniquely zippy, metallic tang, like citrus without the fruit. It was the smell of raw electricity, warm, live and masculine, like lemons and science.

And the room was always silent, apart from the hum.

Kids weren't allowed inside the transmitter station, but we did enter some-times, if Dad was on nightshift, or working alone, or if we were exceptionally bored at home. We could beg to go in and roller skate on the lino in our clunky tin skates. No one would know. Or we could dance to very loud music, alone in the soundproof studio kept for national transmission in case of emergency, but never used, except by us.

Radio stations were encampments in the middle of nowhere, with names indicating the landscape we inhabited: Junction, Pass, Bay. This time we were at Gebbies Pass on Banks Peninsula, so remote we were like crows who had stopped to rest on a radio mast mid-point between Lyttelton and Akaroa. The high summit had one thin and winding access road, leading only to us and flayed by belligerent weather.

Our homes were mapped and belonged to the government, which paid our dads' wages and provided us with houses and gardens and sheds, with gigantic Guy Fawkes bonfires consuming whole trees, and Christmas parties at 3ZB in the city where we would get a bottle of Fanta and Santa would turn up with a present for each kid. Mothers, fathers, babies, kids, kittens, guinea pigs, neighbours—we all belonged to the NZBC, the New Zealand Broadcasting Corporation. We moved from station to station as police and railway families did, but in our case, we moved in a remote and rarefied world, like Himalayan nomads or Mongolian horse people, far removed from any lowland police or railway station.

We lived so far from civilisation we didn't even have to go to church on a Sunday, which made our parents secretly glad. When they weren't working, our dads put down gardens to feed their families. Or they would collect all the station kids and drive us down to Camp Bay to swim or to Birdlings Flat to collect agates, or all the way into Tai Tapu to swim in our concrete school pool. Our mums worked inside. They bathed babies in the kitchen sink, cooked lunch and tea, baked and cleaned, sometimes read a magazine. Mum said that when she was pegging out the washing, she could hear a radio programme humming through the clothesline. Dad said that was just the transmission from the South Pole.

Our high volcanic territory was staked out by a perimeter of giant masts, usually three per station, set out in tripod formation straddling our houses and the neighbouring farms. There was an annexe for storing equipment and a single men's quarters with a tennis court for the young men to thrash out their after-work energy. There were gardens and lawns, roads and paths, old walnut trees and a pine plantation. All life and all formation spread before us as we roller-skated around our mountain kingdom.

Going about my childhood business, I would stop frequently just to gaze, if the view was particularly beautiful that day, perhaps dependent on the hue of light. The hills and the inlets beneath me, winding away towards Governors Bay and Lyttelton, would be framed into perfection by the gap between the trees, with the natural symmetry of the volcano's caldera either shimmering or still in the distance below. The scene was timeless, muted radiance or stark, contrasting colour. I didn't know what to do with the grandeur of such a scene. I wanted to become it—to be the water—to nestle into the nude contours of those hills. I couldn't, so I just absorbed it all into my growing, changing self, like calcium into my teeth and bones. Our landscape held a simmering subterranean volatility never mentioned by the adults.

Big things always happened to mark the year. Fire, snow, lost people, lost animals, heatwaves. Even bushfires from Australia sent their smoke over, encroaching like a fluffy wave of dirty cloud rolling in over the Canterbury Plains towards us, the smoke clouds the same height as our sitting room window. Would it reach us? Would our thin windows be enough to keep out the smoke? We never knew.

We lived so high up, freezing in the winter and sweltering in the summer, that the new TV station in Christchurch used us to measure the highs and lows of the daily temperature. We would race each other to the weather box on the hottest or coldest day to measure the temperature on the long thermometer inside the box and report back to the dads at the station, then wait to hear our number return to us on the evening news, an echo back from the world below.

Dad was also the station's seismograph technician. He measured and recorded the earth's movement, which meant he could disappear from the light and hum of the transmitter building into an underground bunker dug deep into the hillside halfway down towards the bottom mast. The seismograph hut was a dark, musty, one-room prehistoric cave. Only the faintest degree of light was permissible. Inside the cave was one chair and one table. On the table, a large plastic baby bath was filled with chemical fluid and, inside, a submerged roll of photographic paper was secured by wired fingers, which made squiggly lines each time the earth moved, which we couldn't feel but we knew we were living on a volcano, which the adults said was extinct, but you never knew what could happen. It was alive once and what did the squiggly lines mean if the earth wasn't still moving?

I would soon feel repelled by the dankness of the hut and leave Dad to his measuring. Out into the blinding sunlight and up onto the bunker roof, where the black sticky tar-and-turf matting perfectly absorbed my tap dancing. The amphitheatre of the entire Lyttelton basin below was my audience, with Mount

Herbert in the high box seats to my right. There were never any people. Only sheep and tussock to look and wave.

The three radio masts marked out our playground, wide and vast with no adult supervision. Fluted at the base, each mast formed a square, with four feet securely encased into the earth in ugly concrete shoes and rose to a towering pinnacle in an elegant sweep of bright orange steel.

We would try to climb the masts, but the spaces between the steel jambs were so wide and high we had no chance and would just end up swinging pointlessly. We invented other mast games. In winter the ice would drip from the steel beams in long fat stalactites heading down toward the ground. By mid-morning the sun would be releasing daggers of ice from the highest steel struts, slowly falling downward through the air like a brace of arrows. If you looked up through the centre of the mast you could see the lattice of steel rise to a single high apex, its filaments fringed with beautiful white-blue droplets of ice, each being released in turn and dropping from a different place—weapons of slow coldness falling soundlessly through the sky. Sharp, pointy raindrops elongating as they fell.

Was there a sequence to the drop's falling dance? You couldn't stay in one place long enough to find out. Waiting underneath, we would each claim a mast leg, the same way you would mind a base in a softball game, and on the count, we would run to the next base with our faces to the sky, dodging the ice daggers, whooping and yelping as they landed around us. The blitzkrieg of icy danger making us pant and holler with excitement and danger, puffing smoke from our mouths into the cold crisp air, steam rising from our warm bodies as we ripped off coats and hats and gloves, loopy with joy and excess energy and wondering how our mothers could bear to be inside making the beds and chopping the veggies for lunch.

The masts were impressive, and by today's standards, maybe a bit too close to the houses. Perhaps they gave Mum and Dad cancer too early. Who knows?

A version of this essay was previously published as 'Portrait: A radio station childhood' on Newsroom (April 2022): https://www.newsroom.co.nz/memoir-of-a-radio-station

LYNN DAVIDSON

To Travel Somewhere Else

My first travel diary, written when I was nineteen, has a rose pressed inside its pages, like a relic. The diary opens to the page with the disintegrating rose as though the story starts there, with romance. But I know better and turn back to the beginning. I am prepared to give my young self some leeway to be a bit stupid and self-obsessed, but even so, at times it feels like reading *The Secret Diary of Adrian Mole.*

I strain the goodwill of a family friend when she kindly allows me to stay at her home in Kent straight after I arrive in the UK. It is spring, and one day her son visits for tea, which we have outside underneath a spreading oak tree. He finds me appealing and starts taking me out in his car. We go to Canterbury and he shows me his old school in the grounds of Canterbury Cathedral, which my diary records this way:

> *We went to Simon's old school, an enormous posh private school called 'Kings'. Somerset Maugham went there. He also had his ashes scattered there. Of course, the classrooms and 'houses' etc were all enormous old stone places with velvet green lawns and boys walking around in stiff pokey-up white collars and ties, black jackets and stripy trousers. When they go out they wear straw boaters.*

In my passive way, I allow Simon to take me to antique car shows, to his friend John's flat in Holland Park, and to lovely old pubs in the countryside. His mother begins taking me to travel agencies to help organise my next big adventure. In my diary, I think this is because she's regretting the few days of being annoyed with me (I rightly surmise this has something to do with Simon) and has decided to make up for it by being helpful. But clearly, she wants me gone. A New Zealander who has never heard of Kings Canterbury isn't the girl she has in mind for her son. I think of Simon—a charming, slightly plump, fair-haired man with good manners who thought I was diverting and a bit odd. I don't think his mother had anything to worry about.

As I write 'In my passive way,' I think, *but I wasn't passive*. I had left behind friends, over-protective parents, siblings, and the country I knew, to travel alone in Europe. But when it came to the actual travel, I had very few plans. I just failed to think ahead. Part of it was being nineteen, but part was—is— me. Four decades later, I still feel my way forward, almost like a cat whose long whiskers let it know if a shape is big enough to step through. This isn't sensible and probably stems from disbelief in my ability to throw the shape first and then step into it. Or from the belief that there is a next thing that will hold me.

When I read my first travel diary, I'm also amazed at how brave I was, how aware of my sexual power, and how bold I could be. I was quite good at being a teenager, I think, with some surprise. And yet, something was holding me back. On the one hand, I am wandering around Soho, being offered a job in a hippy clothes shop and wondering if I should take it, accepting rides with people I don't know and having inadvisable encounters—all of that ordinary experimental young-person stuff. And on the other hand, I'm writing home to my parents, enquiring about everyone in my extended family and their goings- on as if I were their mother. I even urge my parents to be careful when they embark on a cruise to Rarotonga! What was I doing, playing this slightly sticky solicitous role? I buy presents for everyone, including books, which weigh down my backpack and make 'going home' an actual burden almost from the beginning of my journey. In my letters (which my mother saved for me), I write confidently about something I experienced or saw and then make sure I deflect it with some small slight against myself.

With Simon's mother's assistance, I organise a flight to Amsterdam and land in a backpackers' hostel. I meet two Canadian girls, and we travel together through Germany to Austria, where we end up in Bad Radkersburg, staying with the Omi of one of the girls—her dark house with lace at the windows, the beautiful cakes, the mountains, all very quiet and sepia after the colour and brilliance of Amsterdam. Making up for a few days with barely any food as we made our way there, we eat and eat and eat: Hungarian goulash, schnitzel, ice cream, cakes, Mozart balls, frankfurters in soft buns with lashings of mustard. We go out for dinner, or eat a big dinner with Omi, then go out for coffee and cake, and buy a bottle of wine to drink by the Mur River. One night after dinner,

I play Omi's piano and she hums along. Omi doesn't speak English, but she is sweet and warm and reminds me of my mother.

One day we walk to the border to cross into Yugoslavia (now Slovenia). It is meant to be a day trip to experience the novelty of walking from one country to another and back again, which was the apex of privilege, although I didn't know it then. Well, not initially, anyway.

My Canadian friends get through fine; I don't. First, the border guards tell me my passport has expired when it hasn't. Then they say I must pay for a visa to enter their country. Then they take my passport away into another room and I wait nervously for them to bring it back. Eventually, I am refused entry and don't get to walk across the border with my two friends. It comes down, I think, to the occupation stated in my passport: 'journalist'. Before leaving Wellington, I worked at Press House writing 'fluff' stories in the advertising features department. So, while my friends explore the very edge of Yugoslavia, I spend my time wandering around the very edge of Austria, feeling surprised that I'm not allowed to go where I choose.

I leave Bad Radkersburg and Omi and my Canadian friends to go to Munich, where I stay with an English couple, Emma and Pete, another connection through family friends. I sleep on the couch in Emma and Pete's compact, post-World War II apartment with its small orange balcony facing a street of similar apartment buildings. They ask me if I will stay on to nanny their two-year-old son, Leon—a lively and beautiful fair-haired boy who speaks German-infused English—so that Emma can return to work part-time, and I agree. The couple are old enough to seem proper adults to me and also young enough to party with. There are moments of tension and temper, but there are many more moments of fun. We drive to the mountains and Bavarian villages and go to countless beer gardens. I ask if we can visit Dachau. When we are nearly there, they say it is too late to go to Dachau now, so we go to a pub and have a drink instead. I still don't know if I mind about that or not. Part of me (perhaps a cowardly part) is grateful that my nineteen-year-old self was spared the experience.

We often sit up late talking about Hitler and Germany and New Zealand and religion. We listen to Pink Floyd and The Rolling Stones and watch Monty Python movies, or, when Pete has gone to bed, Emma and I watch sad movies like the one about the priest who saves orphans in Mexico. Their German friend, Hans, turns up early one morning and I am still in bed on the couch. I hear the knock and Pete getting out of bed to let him in. They come quietly into the lounge to get to the kitchen to make coffee, and I hear Hans pause beside my bed and indicate to Pete that he thinks I look good. Pete agrees but sounds embarrassed. Hans is my father's age.

One day, when Emma, Leon and I are in the city, a German woman comes up to Emma and asks if she would like to earn money trying cosmetics. The woman gives Emma a card and invites her to a meeting later that day to find out more. In a picturesque square, there is a man playing a piano accordion, and a little girl playing a tiny cello, and a young man dressed in white playing a recorder. There are fruit stalls piled high with cherries and strawberries. I am suddenly very tired—I feel like I am hallucinating all of this. I am also exhausted by the straightforwardness of Germans. How they carry their bodies in their words and always get just a little bit too close when they share their opinions or ask something. Germans, I know, are comfortable with nakedness. I can imagine that this is because clothes might be felt to soften the very fleshy embodiedness of their interactions. It is so strange to me, the formality and the fleshiness. I think of Katherine Mansfield's story 'Germans At Meat':

> Bread soup was placed upon the table. 'Ah,' said the Herr Rat, leaning upon the table as he peered into the tureen, 'that is what I need. My 'magen' has not been in order for several days. Bread soup, and just the right consistency. I am a good cook myself'—he turned to me.
>
> 'How interesting,' I said, attempting to infuse just the right amount of enthusiasm into my voice.

Emma and I go to a guesthouse where the woman who wanted Emma to try cosmetics embarks on a long talk. We drink some free beer, figure there are no free makeup samples on offer, and use Leon as an excuse to leave to make our way home. It was strange that the woman had approached Emma and strange that we had decided to go. Sometimes Emma feels like a beautiful older sister who burns for a bigger life. She takes me with her on adventures just because I am there.

The next day Emma and I cycle into the Black Forest. Emma has Leon on her bike. Among the tall pines and firs are deer and squirrels and little wild strawberries. We stop at a guesthouse for beer, cigarettes and chocolate. Leon runs around the tables and other customers make their displeasure clear by telling us about it. Emma flares up and asks them if they were ever children.

Emma and Pete ask if I'd like to come with them on a three-week holiday to Turkey. They will take their camper van, and Hans will take his; he will be travelling with two of his daughters. I desperately want to see Turkey.

We visit Hans and his wife, Jan, in their old whitewashed farmhouse, which sits among rolling hills and forest about three hours out of Munich. One room in their house has floor-to-ceiling shelves of books in German and English, classical music cassettes and records. One of Hans's albums is a recording of Hitler's speeches. On its cover, Hitler sits in a chair with a blonde-haired little girl on his lap. Hans is an antique dealer, so the house is full of fascinating and lovely things. He has two parrots who sit on his shoulders and eat food from his mouth. We have dinner by candlelight at a long wooden table. They are, I say in my diary, 'health food freaks'. We have stuffed red peppers and a brown rice salad. We stay the night; my room is a low-roofed bedroom at the top of a set of narrow stairs. Jan, is an English woman. She's younger than him and seems both sad and angry most of the time. Her face has a hectic look to it. Perhaps my face looked like that many years later when I, too, was in an impossible relationship that had some unarguably beautiful architecture around it. The next morning, Jan, Emma, Leon and Jan's little girl Julia and I walk to a nearby village in a picturesque valley. There is a shop that looks like a house. It is a bakery with just one bun and a flower in the window. I look at it for a while and feel hungry. I think it's the best window display I have ever seen. There are women in long black dresses and shawls forking hay in fields. There are window boxes and old people sitting outside their houses enjoying the June sun. We are close to the Czechoslovakian and Austrian borders. It is still odd and exciting to me to look across the land towards borders that magic up other countries. Back at the farmhouse, Hans and Jan argue and keep arguing until the following day, when we leave for Munich.

I try to ring Mum on her birthday but can't get an answer. I try again and again and then find out that my grandad, the Scottish one, has died. I am sad but relieved for him; he was so bored living in the old people's home in Tauranga. It's hard not to be home, not to go to his funeral.

We are approaching the end of summer, and I'm starting to feel claustrophobic in the little apartment in Munich. I get a heavy cold and decide that I need to move on. Much as I like Leon and his funny ways (singing heartfully along to the theme song of a *Heidi* cartoon in German and English), I'm bored sitting around in the apartment while Emma goes out to work. Emma wants me to stay on as Leon's nanny after Turkey, but I don't want to. Hans and Jan come to visit, and Jan and Emma have a fight, during which Jan throws four glasses at Emma. I go to Zurich for a break and meet an Australian guy who tells me he smuggles cars into Istanbul and who shows me around Zurich.

Then I write in my diary about driving with Hans through Basel in northwestern Switzerland across the border into France to put petrol in his camper van because it was cheaper there. I don't remember this well, but I think Hans drove me to or from Zurich. No doubt he was doing some trade there, but I wonder why anyone thought this was a good idea—including me. We spend a couple of days travelling together. We talk a lot and passionately—he is a very passionate man who cries and flares up easily. He wants to take me to North Africa. He lends me an expensive SLR camera and says he can get the prints done for free. He gives me a rose, which I press between the pages of my diary. I write that 'nothing happened' and that 'it's going to be a hassle in Turkey with Hans, I think'.

We leave for our trip to Turkey, our two large and well-equipped camper vans in convoy through the Austrian mountains into Italy, where I feel a weight lift from me. I love Italy, its craggy mountains with cypress and olive trees, the scruffy villages so different from the picture-postcard German, Swiss and Austrian villages. I like the windy country roads that remind me of New Zealand. All of us relax. We leave northern Italy and begin the long drive through the centre of Yugoslavia. Hans and I are often the last two awake, sitting outside in this beautiful and bare-feeling land, talking and talking and talking.

The further we drive into Yugoslavia, the further we seem to move back in time. There are peasants in long dresses and scarves, and horses and carts, and old shepherds with small flocks of sheep, and children everywhere asking for cigarettes. On the roadsides, there are lonely and fragrant fruit stands. On the endless stretches of road are billboards with Tito's serious and beloved face on them. We drive long days and sometimes through the night. We travel on and on, through the long central transit road of Yugoslavia, me sleeping in a tent with Hans's daughter, who looks at me funny, not in dislike, but as though we share a secret. Sometimes she smiles a small smile. She is from Hans's second marriage and I don't think she likes Jan, the third wife, so maybe in her mind, we are accomplices in undermining her. Sometimes we swim together in rivers. In our tent, she sleeps with a gun close to her pillow to scare off wild dogs.

We travel through Skopje and camp by the Vardar River, close to the Greek border. That night Hans and Pete go to bed before Emma and me. We sit up late, Emma teaching me some German. I am relieved to get to the sea at Thessaloniki, where I sit by myself, looking out at the ocean. I say in my diary that 'there is a bit of tension among us all at the moment', and I think by this point, I have started sleeping with Hans.

I imagine, or tell myself, that Emma and Pete don't know what we are doing, but maybe they do, and although neither of them much like Hans's unhappy wife, I doubt they would have felt comfortable with this. Relationships between the two couples are volatile and I don't understand them. The four glasses that Jan threw at Emma no doubt carried plenty of old pain, old stories. Perhaps Emma knows and Pete suspects. Although, given that they've known Hans across years and marriages, why would they not imagine that this could happen?

I am blindly, wilfully outside of time. I am sleeping with a charming man whose home holds hundreds of books and walls full of gorgeous classical music (forget about that one album with the blonde girl on it). We get each other, I think (we absolutely don't). He tells me he likes me with my long curly hair tied back. He supports me when Emma is angry with me for something. I am young and, although not blameless, certainly naïve. And hungry. I am loving being out in the world. Sitting outside until the stars brighten, cloaking the bare hills, then fading into pink and orange skies. Hans takes offence easily. He likes me in my floaty hippy dresses, but I'm more comfortable in cut-off jeans. I would almost give my right arm to keep the freedom I am enjoying. I am one of his treasures.

I write in my diary that I never want to leave Turkey. Because Hans, Pete and Emma have travelled there often, they know it well, so we go off the beaten track. A huge orange sun sets nightly into the Marmara Sea, the Black Sea, and the Aegean. We cross the Bosphorus from Thrace to Anatolia. From Europe to Asia. Late one night, Hans drives us to see the shining mosques of Istanbul. I write in my diary that mosques, especially at night, must have the most beautiful architecture in the world.

*

Years later, but not so many, maybe seven, when I am married and a mother, we visit Emma and Pete in Munich. They talk about Hans and how he killed himself. A gun in his mouth. It happened just before we left New Zealand, but my parents didn't tell me for fear of upsetting me when we were just heading off (my mother had guessed there was something between Hans and me). Anyway, they didn't say, and so I hear it there, where I first met him. It is winter in Munich and everything is frozen, including the fountains: the water frozen in its flow between slim upraised arms, small bare breasts, fish, mermaids, gargoyles, and the bowl for catching and releasing. I think of the record with Hitler and the little girl on its cover. We leave Emma and Pete's and go to the München Hauptbahnhof to travel somewhere else, and I get a terrible migraine and a kind German doctor looks after me.

REFERENCE
Bread soup was placed upon … Katherine Mansfield, 'Germans At Meat', from *In a German Pension* (Stephen Swift & Co Ltd, 1911).

How to Shuck an Oyster

I'm learning how to eat oysters off the rocks at Ti Point.

My mum and I crouch at the entrance of a flat expanse of grey rockpools near the southern end of the beach. The rocks stretch out to sea, towards Te Hauturu-o-Toi (Little Barrier) on the horizon of the Hauraki Gulf. Waves crash white foam over their craggy ends. Mossy pools pocket the rock's surface, exposed in low tide. Communities of lacquered black barnacles glisten in the mid-afternoon sun.

The oysters are clustered around the rocks on the edge of the sand, their shells mottled with shades of purple and white, rimmed in a charcoal black. I know not to step on their sharp edges with my bare feet, but in this moment, they don't look harmful. They sparkle with a gloss of seawater.

Our feet sink gently into the sand as we crouch to their level. I watch my mum tap around the edges of an oyster's jagged shell with a small rock, slowly nudging away the shellfish's protection. She is gentle, taking her time. *Tap-tap-tap-tap-tap.* The top layer suddenly comes loose, exposing creamy silvery flesh. She carefully slides it out of the shell and hands it to me to taste. Assuming I won't enjoy it, I grimace and swallow the oyster fast. I'm surprised by the fresh, smooth aftertaste. It tastes good. My mouth feels clean.

I want to try again.

My mum hands me the rock. I pick out the largest oyster in a tight, dense cluster of shells and start to tap. My enthusiasm is excessive, and I pound too hard, accidentally smashing in the rim. *Crunch.* The oyster now looks inedible, splintered with fragments of purple shell. I'm horrified at cutting the oyster's life short.

'It's alright. Here. You can wash it in the sea.'

Mum scoops it up and lets a wave wash over her fingers. It sweeps away the sand and shell, restoring the oyster to an edible form.

I eat slowly this time, paying close attention to how the oyster feels and tastes. The flesh is slippery and smooth. The taste is tender and sweet from the sea, with a pop of creaminess. There's only the faintest hint of salt.

'Aren't they delicious?' she asks me. I nod. I'm starting to understand why she loves them.

We eat a few more that afternoon, as the tide drifts back in and our togs dry in the sun, but only a few. 'You shouldn't take too many at once,' my mum says, 'it's important to let them grow and take only your share.'

*

This love for oysters is inherited. My grandmother famously ate them off the same rocks while pregnant (although the sea was likely cleaner back then), and I have never seen my mother refuse an oyster. My siblings and I eat oysters with our parents now on special occasions. We share trays of a dozen Pacific oysters from the Asian fish market down the road, the shells resting on styrofoam rather than rock.

We are purists—firmly refusing tempura or a heavy sauce, in favour of cracked black pepper, a squirt of lemon and drops of Kaitaia Fire. The native rock oysters at Ti Point have ruined my tolerance for oysters that aren't startlingly fresh.

Sometimes my grandparents appeared in the doorway of the cottages at Ti Point with shucked Pacific oysters from a roadside shack near Matakana. I'd watch them eat the oysters straight out of the punnet with my parents as a mid-afternoon snack in the sun. The oysters were enormous, triple the size of those on the beach. It was strange to see oysters so naked.

I crave the sweet freshness of the rock oysters and the reward after shucking one yourself.

My family's taste for and access to oysters at Ti Point are some of the many benefits we've inherited from my ancestor who settled there in the nineteenth century. However, to these shellfish, we are newcomers.

Around the corner from the beach, beyond the headland hosting the remains of an ancient pā, is Te Kohuroa (Mathesons Bay). In this bay, if you know where to look, the rocks are packed with the fossilised remains of ancient oysters, millions of years old, their shells reportedly the size of bread-and-butter plates.

Scattered among these remains are the native rock oysters we now eat. They are only found along the northeastern tip of Te Ika-a-Māui (the North Island). Other shellfish attach themselves to surfaces with a small foot. These oysters stubbornly fuse half of themselves onto rocks. In te reo Māori, these native oysters are called tio repe. Tio also means freezing cold.

When I was younger, we often walked down the dusty gravel road tracing the peninsula's spine to the bay on the opposite side of the point. As we explored the calmer coastline of the Whangateau Harbour, examining rocks and shells, my mum pointed out exposed parts of dark soil densely peppered with fine layers of white shell. She told us they were records of where Māori— Ngāti Manuhiri—used to live and gather the once abundant shellfish. We called these middens 'pipi banks' and spotted them everywhere as we walked, under pōhutukawa roots or fence posts. We understood not to touch or climb on them. They were to be respected.

In my beginner te reo Māori classes we practised our mihimihi.

Nō Kotimana, nō Ingarangi ōku tūpuna
My ancestors are from Scotland and England
Nō Tāmaki Makaurau ahau
I am from Auckland

Describing myself as from Tāmaki Makaurau is accurate, but it also feels incomplete. Ti Point offers me such a strong sense of identity. So, one day, using the kaiako's template, I included the phrase:

Ko Ti Point taku tūrangawaewae
Ti Point is my standing place

The kaiako was confused.

'Kei hea a Ti Point? Ti Point? What on earth does Ti Point mean?'

I explained it's a small peninsula north of Tāmaki Makaurau, between Leigh and Omaha. She told me to research it for next week.

'I've already tried,' I mumbled.

She paused, thinking to herself.

'Why don't you say Tī Kōuka instead. Tī generally means cabbage tree. Are there lots of cabbage trees there?'

'Not really,' I replied.

There are some tī kōuka at the edge of the lawn by the white gate marking the steep path down to the beach. Their bushy tops seem to float in the blue sea behind, brushing the Coromandel Peninsula floating in a haze on the horizon.

'Maybe there were lots of tī kōuka in the beginning,' the kaiako suggested.

Ti Point is covered in mānuka. I've wondered whether the name is a hybrid of 'tea trees', which my mother says my great-grandmother, who was born at Ti Point, called them. The native bush has grown back thick and fast, recovering after fire cleared the land in previous centuries. Alongside kauri and toetoe, the mānuka form a dense, bristly protective circle around the two cottages sitting high on a platform of land above the sea. The trees bolster slopes so steep, the sea bowls in out of sight, its presence marked by audible crashes. The track to the beach is thin and rugged, loosely looping down the slope. Even when overgrown, we can instinctively follow its turns through pōhutakawa roots and branches.

At first, our parents carried my cousins and me down and back up again. As we got older, we scrambled down the slope on our own. We'd burst onto the beach, surprising the resident oystercatchers, our legs etched in bright red lines from gorse and cutty grass lining the track, casting aside our towels, abandoning our shoes, and running over burning hot sand towards the sea, to the rockpools.

We still throw ourselves into the surf uninhibited by rocks at the northern end, pressing against the sand as waves roll heavily above. We trace colourful curves of shells along the high-tide mark, searching for intact kina and translucent slices of yellow cornflake shell. We inspect cat's eyes, shrimp and hermit crabs in the rockpools at the southern end, studying crevices for the claws of purple-shelled crabs. We always sit in the same spot, in the middle of the beach, under ancient, long spindly branches of the pōhutukawa that protects my family's pale blend of English and Scottish skin.

The beach's restricted access means we are often alone. We watch boats attempt to land, floating over stretches of rocks they can't see but we can.

It can feel as though we know these rockpools, tides and oystercatchers better than anyone. To us, it is the most beautiful place in the world.

Sometimes as an adult, interpretations of the world you held onto as a child lose their foundations.

*

When I was small, I asked my grandmother where cat's eyes went when they disappeared into their shells. 'That's their house,' she said, pointing at the blue-green pearly door.

I imagined the cat's eyes retreating to a small living room with a bed, dining table and chairs, and kitchen in the corner, like those in the cottages. I unquestioningly conjured this image until, one day, my twenty-six-year-old self suddenly realised it was a fantasy while examining the Ti Point rockpools alone. I'd imposed the idea of my world onto these tiny shellfish. I felt embarrassed for never questioning it.

Growing up, I didn't question the stories of how my family developed a relationship with Ti Point. For as long as I can remember, I've heard about my ancestor, William Torkington—a widowed carpenter from England whose wife and daughters died from influenza—walking over eighty kilometres north from Tāmaki Makaurau to Ti Point, seeking land and a better life for his three teenage sons. I imagine him with a walking stick, like the ones my grandfather whittled down from mānuka branches to help him down to the beach.

When my ancestor (my great-great-great-grandfather on my mother's side) arrived at Ti Point, he purchased a land title covering most of the small peninsula. If you walk down the road to the wharf now, the name Torkington is still printed on many letterboxes.

My grandmother has described the peninsula as having been 'abandoned', deemed tapu after a Māori battle on the beach. The origins of this story are unclear, probably handed down to her, too. My mum and I tested the validity of this story as we respectively learned about New Zealand history at university. We speculated whether Hongi Hika passed through the area during the musket wars, but the timing doesn't make sense; the wars were decades before my ancestor arrived.

Also clashing against and undermining the word 'abandoned' are other family stories about Māori women looking after Torkington's sons while he went back to the city, or preparing food in the bay down the road, boiling water in pots over a fire on the sand.

As my knowledge about te ao Māori and our country's fraught history expanded, my mistrust in the idea Ti Point was free for the taking grew. My limited understanding of tapu told me its presence indicated a strong, protective relationship—the opposite of any absence or abandonment.

I started to understand we've been holding onto interpretations of events, not unquestionable truths. Deep down, I knew others have loved the rockpools, too—mana whenua, who established a relationship with this land long before us, and who might be able to tell me what the 'Ti' in 'Ti Point' really means.

Although my questioning increased, I still clung to my family's stories, like an oyster to its rock, reluctant to let go of how they shaped my understanding of Ti Point and my family.

*

Many people approach eating an oyster for the first time with suspicion. Cultural assumptions tell their palates these shellfish are slimy and unlikeable, a threat to their culinary sensibilities. In the nineteenth century, oysters were an abundant everyday food easily gathered from the shoreline in both Aotearoa and the United Kingdom. Oysters now represent luxury, and I've encountered a strange defensive superiority from some who choose *not* to eat them.

Yet often, the oyster derails people's assumptions, and they want to try more. There is even a sense of pride in overcoming a mental hurdle.

Oysters are deceptively complicated—tender, sharp and resilient, with a sensitive nervous system that impulsively slams shut when they sense a threat. It's an impulse humans share. We attach ourselves to shields of protection, avoiding exposure to confrontation, carrying a sense of displacement.

Conversations on decolonisation and our relationships to land in Aotearoa tend to summon similar trepidation. Rather than pushing ourselves into discomfort, it's easier to assume asking questions or openly discussing colonisation is threatening. Discussions are stonewalled before they even start.

In her essay 'Pākehā and doing the work of decolonisation', Pākehā environmental studies academic Amanda Thomas writes:

> *A Pākehā sense of identity is focused on connection to the land, but it's also based on actively ignoring how we came to be connected to that land (our collective history). For many Pākehā, we're almost proud if we don't know who our ancestors are and how they came here.*

I've tended to say I don't know exactly how my family came to be at Ti Point, I don't know how my ancestor came to hold legal title recognised by those who held the balance of power.

To say I simply didn't know kept me in a comfortable space. I didn't want to know in case knowledge would undermine my own emotional connection. Each time I decided to investigate further or ask more questions, including from family members who could tell me more, my discomfort manifested in hesitation and then inaction.

My initial searches for information online were cursory, tailored to suit my own relationship with the land. I searched the Ngāti Manuhiri deed of settlement for references to 'Ti Point'. I took the lack of results as evidence Ti Point was somehow excluded, divorced from the land surrounding it over which Ngāti Manuhiri are mana whenua. I closed the document without reading further, ignoring the nagging warning that this was inadequate.

In other spaces—at work, with friends, online, in te reo Māori classes—I was frustrated by Pākehā nervousness around our capacity to meaningfully engage with te ao Māori. Standing in the kitchen at work, a colleague and I talked at length about how to encourage people to embrace the discomfort of having honest, interrogating conversations.

However, I ignored the implications of my connections with Ti Point. There were emotional walls between my desire for greater accountability, and putting it into practice, that I didn't want to climb.

*

One afternoon, I watched a protest calling for Māori land at Ihumātao in Tāmaki Makaurau to be returned to tangata whenua. It was a bright, high-blue sky day. Bus drivers stood in the street, abandoning their immobile buses. A crowd of curious public servants formed a circle around kneeling protestors.

The peaceful, silent protest filled the Lambton Quay and Bowen Street intersection beneath Parliament. Orange smoke floated between tino rangatiratanga flags and a large sign declaring FLETCHERS RETURN THE WHENUA. The protesters sang 'Tūtira Mai Ngā Iwi'.

The previous day, a group occupying land at Ihumātao in Māngere fighting for recognition of its historical, cultural and archaeological value, had been served an eviction notice. The land sits next to the Ōtuataua Stonefields Historic Reserve where lines of curated stone walls are evidence of Aotearoa's earliest market gardens.

In July 1863, the land was stolen from mana whenua by British and New Zealand troops, then later sold to a Pākehā family. The confiscation was justified by alleging mana whenua, who were growing crops to feed Tāmaki Makaurau, had refused to pledge allegiance to 'the Crown'. In 2014, the Auckland Council earmarked the land for a housing development, to be built by Fletcher Building.

Protests across the motu supporting the return of Ihumātao to tangata whenua in the twenty-first century were described as a repeat of Bastion Point. A repeat of Parihaka. A repeat of Rangiaowhia. An exposure of the painful need for symbiotic relationships between cultural frameworks and values.

Fletchers argued Ihumātao was different because it was private land. Right-wing political parties argued government intervention would meddle in 'private property rights'. However, 'private property rights' is attractive for its simplicity. It skims over the complicated web of competing rights, interests and connections to place that transcend any perceived legitimacy of title. It ignores how legal title reflects contestable value-sets and systems. At law school, we learned private property rights are deeply ideological—a historical phenomenon premised on imperialist systems, assertions of power and centring of individual rights—and a feature Aotearoa inherited from the United Kingdom.

'Ihumātao makes me think about Ti Point,' I said to my mum on the phone, after telling her about the protest.

'I've been wondering about that, too,' she replied.

While the sand of the beach and the rockpools are intrinsic parts of our identities, they've never been exclusively ours. We enjoy them as beneficiaries of colonisation. We access natural resources on the beach due to a private legal title recognised by a colonial government.

William Torkington's intentions were to seek a better life for his family. However, whether he knew it at the time, purchasing land made him an active participant in the colonising effort that alienated Ngāti Manuhiri. People might argue they are not responsible for the actions of their ancestors. Yet, as these historical events continue to grant us benefits, they continue to have destructive effects on tangata whenua.

Forty-eight hours after the eviction notice was served, hundreds of people gathered at Ihumātao. Images declaring solidarity filled my social media feeds with the words *tino rangatiratanga never ceded*.

I pictured the Māori woman from stories handed down to me, in the bay on the Ti Point peninsula boiling water for cockles, with pipi banks illuminated in the sun behind her.

Ihumātao is stolen land.

Ti Point may be stolen land.

*

I tried researching Ti Point again.

Tap.

My searches retrieved Auckland Regional Council documents for a study of the Whangateau Harbour. They detailed an 'early settlers' observation of the dominance of mānuka on the Ti Point peninsula from 1863, indicating the bush had been cleared for Māori settlement of the area. Mānuka is one of the first plants to regenerate on cleared land.

The document went on to say, 'Early settlement of the Whangateau catchment was primarily influenced by the requirement for easy access to the harbour, reflected by the predominance of recorded Māori archaeological sites at coastal locations including Ti Point.'

Tap.

I searched for 'Ti Point' in the New Zealand Gazette on the Land Information New Zealand website. Information on Ti Point was limited, but descriptions of Te Kohuroa were more detailed. The website said, 'In the early nineteenth century Te Kohuroa was also the site of a major battle involving Ngāti Manuhiri after a sacred place there was despoiled by a visiting party (Native Land Court, Kaipara Minute Book 4, February 1884).'

Tap.

I read the Ngāti Manuhiri deed of settlement documents, properly this time, knowing the information gathered for the settlement process would be thorough. On page 14, I came across the words 'Hāwera (Tī Point)'. On *Te Aka Māori Dictionary*, 'hāwera' means a place where the fern or bush was destroyed by fire.

Tap.

Seal colonies lived on the rocks at Ti Point, before land was cleared.

Tap.

In 1841, the Crown purchased an extensive area called 'Mahurangi and Omaha' where Ngāti Manuhiri had customary interests and an important ancestral relationship. The Crown relied on information from vendors who were not from the iwi and Ngāti Manuhiri were not consulted on the sales. A decade later, the Crown recognised Ngāti Manuhiri interests in the land. But by then, settlers were moving into the area—my ancestor included—and sales of land continued.

Tap.

A map shows Ngāti Manuhiri's affiliation with the coastal marine area. It extends along the eastern coast from Bream Tail to Whangaparāoa, then out to Te Hauturu-o-Toi. Ti Point is squarely in the middle.

Tap.

The Whangateau Harbour boasts the remains of six fortified pā.

Tap.

In 1840, mana whenua held customary interests over approximately 250,000 acres of land. In the 1890s, they held ten percent, losing access to natural resources along the eastern coastline that supported their way of life and identity.

In the twenty-first century, as my family continue to visit Ti Point, Ngāti Manuhiri are effectively landless.

Tap.

*

When the tide is out in the Whangateau Harbour, the expanse between Ti Point and the Omaha sandspit transforms into a huge stretch of sand webbed with threads of the sea.

We used to collect cockles here, alongside Ngāti Manuhiri. Armed with buckets and bucket hats, my family members would slowly scatter themselves across the bay in the rich sun, as we traced random paths of shellfish, searching for ribbed shells of bulbous cockles with our fingers and toes. I remember other families there too, with buckets or sacks. The sandflats were so expansive we could all collect the shellfish comfortably side by side.

In an interview on *E-Tangata*, Māori academic Leonie Pihama writes:

I don't believe our tūpuna had an issue about sharing whenua. The issue is about control and power and who gets to determine the way we may operate as a country. We've always had embedded within te ao Māori a practice of manaakitanga.

My family's emotional attachment to Ti Point accompanies a strong desire to offer it protection. I think my family can be proud of their care for it. The native bush has regenerated, full of birds and wildlife. My grandparents have devoted countless years to looking after trees or picking rubbish off the beach, among many other acts of care I'm not aware of. My cousins and I talk about what we can do—removing pine trees and culling invasive species.

As a new generation has reached adulthood, we are increasingly thinking about Ti Point's future. I hope we continue to thoughtfully interrogate what our relationship to this coastline means for future generations—not only ours but those of the communities in the area, including Ngāti Manuhiri. I hope we embrace opportunities for repair.

Apparently, Torkington's son, my great-great-grandfather, preferred to read Marxist texts than look after a farm. In my immediate and extended family members now, there are similar streaks of a fierce social conscience. I suspect our ancestors would be proud to see us harness our principles in untangling ongoing impacts of inherited colonisation and connections with the land, particularly for tangata whenua.

As Moana Jackson writes, decolonisation is unconcerned with limiting the potential of relationships. Instead, it seeks balancing through restoration by offering a chance to reach for 'future flowerings' of truth and justice. He writes 'in giving back to Māori the right of self-determination, it offers everyone a place to stand.'

*

The sun feels fierce on my bare back. I wonder if I have enough sunblock on. My arms shine with salt from the sea.

The sand's contours on the beach are never the same when we pay a visit. A recent storm flattened out the sand in the lower tideline, exposing more rockpools than usual.

The smooth rock in my hand has a comforting weight. The oyster I've chosen is in the middle of a cluster of oysters. I practise what my mum has taught me and knock gently around the shell, trying to treat the oyster with respect.

Shucking an oyster teaches assertiveness, self-awareness and kindness. Prising open the protective shield around my family's relationship with Ti Point will need a similar approach of concerted effort and care for all involved. It will need forceful gentleness.

The shell of the oyster shifts and lifts open.

REFERENCES

A Pākehā sense of identity ... Amanda Thomas, 'Pākehā and doing the work of decolonisation', in *Imagining Decolonisation* (BWB Texts, 2020).

I don't believe our tūpuna ... Leonie Pihama, *E-Tangata*, 1 July 2018: https://e-tangata.co.nz/korero/leonie-pihama-lets-start-by-returning-the-waitara-land/

JESS DUCEY

Securitising Gender

It's unfair how beautiful the city is at night.

After yet another marathon of *The L Word*—when I first came out, Fiona made it her mission to catch me up on the queer media I'd overlooked in my decades of tragically misguided heterosexuality—I nursed my third 'just one' whisky nightcap and pondered how to get home. I'd missed the last bus, and it's a leisurely three kilometres from hers back to mine, through the tunnel and past the war memorial. It was one of those cloudy nights in early summer, where the moon is full, the air turns cool, and the wind dies down to a pleasant salt-scented breeze that reminds you that this city is surrounded by the sea. Perfect for an evening stroll, except for the whole sporadically lit suburbs situation.

We stood there, two strong independent women, debating whether I should walk or call a taxi. Fi said that, in my place, she would almost certainly walk but felt weird suggesting it to someone else. As a staunch public transit enthusiast and former member of the council's cycleways team (not to mention a cheap bastard), so would I—except for that nagging voice that sounds like a *New Zealand Herald* commenter hissing, 'Well, what did you expect at that hour?'

I know that I would be seen as culpable in my own rape or murder, and that is somehow more terrifying than the act itself. I suppose it's a rational response—there's only a moderate risk I'll actually be attacked, but it's a near certainty that if I am, I'll be blamed for it.

We jokingly assessed which of us was more intimidating and less of a target—she has the long, lithe body of a runner, whereas I am all tits and ass and soft belly. Would she pass as an innocuous man in dim light? She could outrun them, but I could sit on them. Or eat them. Humour is a fucked-up way of dealing with a world that hates you, but it's all we have.

I fill my water bottle 'in case I get thirsty on the arduous journey through the suburbs' but really so there would be something heavy in my bag. I don't drive and all my offices are swipecard access, so I only have one key to carry between my fingers. I stick one headphone in, drop the cord down my shirt, put the music on low so I won't be oblivious to my surroundings, and march out the door. Confidently, but not urgently.

*

As a teenager, I had a dance teacher who insisted that a tiny movement or glance could convey more than the most perfectly executed series of fouettés en tournant. Like me, he loved ballet but could barely touch his toes, so he gifted me his passion for contemporary dance, where we could make up for our physical shortcomings with all of our feelings.

What sort of stride says I know where I am going and someone is waiting for me? What arm position suggests that I am listening to Courtney Barnett sing *I want to walk through the park in the dark* and I know how to kick where it hurts? At what angle should I hold my head to convey that I am not afraid but also not so confident as to be asking to be taken down a peg or five?

*

According to the constructivist school of international relations, securitisation is the process by which something is manipulated into an issue of national security, usually to justify extreme policies or actions. Say, the way a politician might manufacture stories about murderous asylum seekers to condone putting children in cages, or a government might fixate on Islamic terrorism while entitled white men gun down civilians—just hypotheticals.

As postgraduate students, we mocked it for being a wanky way of describing what feels obvious, especially with the benefit of hindsight. Securitisation is just a name given to the way the powerful make their worldview the norm and everyone else the troublesome other.

I think about the constructivists every time a man rolls his eyes when I talk about gender. A colleague once smugly told me that he transcended identity politics. He didn't see gender, or race, or sexuality, and he pitied people who couldn't move past it.

Like me, was the implication.

*

I hate every single asshole who honks in the Mt Victoria tunnel with the fire of a thousand suns. The honks are allegedly to scare off a ghost. In life, that ghost was Phyllis Avis Symons, a seventeen-year-old girl whose 'boyfriend'—a man fourteen years her senior—knocked her unconscious and buried her alive after he got her pregnant in 1931.

If this was fiction, an editor would tell me to tone down the overwrought metaphor.

I think about Phyllis every time I pass through that tunnel: who she might have become if her body and her sexuality had belonged to her, her favourite colour, what she wanted to be when she grew up, whether she preferred pie or cake, if she kept a cat; had she ever had an orgasm or did he just lie and flatter his way into using her body for his own pleasure?

*

Sometimes I wonder who I would be if my womanness mattered less, or was just less prominent. I'm soft, all curves and no angles, thick thighs, breasts round and hips wide, with the enormous eyes of a clown or cartoon Disney princess, depending on the viewer's fondness for me. Not necessarily feminine, but female, any way you cut it, even in my butchest clothes.

The modern notion of androgyny is a flat chest and sad eyes and murderous cheekbones in finely tailored menswear. I have none of those, and while I wouldn't mind the cheekbones, I'm really only interested in a herringbone blazer with perfectly placed bust darts.

A few years ago, a colleague used they/them pronouns for me at an event and I never corrected her. I was barely out as bisexual, a year away from that first tiny gateway undercut. I have thought about that evening at least once a week ever since, wondering why my overwhelming memory is one of being deeply flattered.

*

A man on a road bike approaches, sees me, slows his pace. His face is pleasantly neutral but not overly friendly, and he makes eye contact to make sure that I am not surprised by his sudden appearance. He thanks me when I press myself against the tunnel wall to let him pass, and I think about the laughable approach to urban design that can call this a 'shared path' with a straight face.

*

Every few months, I think that maybe I want to try a binder, and then I remember Daniel Laver's 2017 review and accompanying tweet:

> my only other piece of advice, if you get a binder, is to sternly tell it 'This better not awaken anything in me' before putting it on

Do I actually want a body without breasts, or do I just want to know what it feels like to be invisible? Or maybe I just wish I could walk out of a thrift store with the tweed wardrobe of the eccentric history professor I sometimes see when I look at myself in a mirror.

Is this dysphoria, or does a lifetime of diet culture and disordered eating mean I default to thinking my body is the cause of all of life's dilemmas, that everything would be easier if it would just fall in line and behave?

*

I once estimated the tens of thousands of hours I'd spent hating my body and trying to will it into an unattainable ideal—enough to learn a language or a musical instrument, surely—but that's only the beginning of accounting for the costs of a female body.

The money spent on taxi rides in less familiar cities. The therapy. The booze. Running emails and texts by the group chat to make sure I don't sound like a hateful harpy or a vapid ditz. Trying on a half dozen outfits to strike the right balance of fun but professional, attractive but not slutty, demure but not prudish, confident but not arrogant. Learning to sit correctly. Shaving, waxing, cutting, curling, straightening, dyeing, obsessing over the various hairs on my body.

For the first year or so after I quit shaving, I spent most of the time I'd saved worrying about whether people were judging me instead of revelling in the wind blowing through my leg hair. Securitisation turns every facet of existence into a political act. It's exhausting, and my body isn't even that political.

*

A man so drunk he can't walk straight stumbles along the footpath outside the closed bottle shop, oblivious to me, the shrubs in the landscaping, and the lamppost at the pedestrian crossing. I stop at Pukeahu to admire the stained glass in one of the statues, taking shitty phone photos to prove to myself that this is just as much my park as anyone else's and, damn it, I can sit here at 1am if I want.

Three teenage boys walk by, talking about the surprise windfall of their holiday pay and the hilariously large and smelly shit one of their flatmates took. They do not notice me.

*

The further I get into queerness, the less attached I am to any idea of womanhood. I cut my feminist teeth in reproductive rights activism, but I've never wanted to birth children and went fifteen years without menstruating.

My work, my hobbies, my values, my entire identity hinges on sticking it to the patriarchy. I was a model student—I thrive on external validation—but years of being good 'for a girl' at maths and science and just plain good at literature and history led me down the humanities path. So, here I am, perpetually overanalysing whether I've actually chosen any part of my identity.

Would I feel more womanly if I had any interest in using my biological destiny? How much of my identity as a fat feminist woman is just because that's what you see when you look at me?

Despite the fifteen-year ovulation hiatus, I still carry tampons because of a YouTube makeup tutorial where a trans woman talked about the quiet beauty of moments of solidarity in women's toilets, whether it's drunk strangers telling each other how beautiful they are, or passing a tampon under the door, or encouraging a crying woman with smeared mascara to dump him.

Maybe that's all womanhood really is—finding little ways to help each other stick it to the patriarchy.

*

I finally order the binder. Cropped, in grey to hide stains, per Lavery's recommendation. It takes ages to arrive, then sits in the closet for a few months, where I occasionally take it out, gently touch its unyielding fabric, and warn it not to overturn my life.

At last, I muster up the courage to try it on, wriggling awkwardly as I arrange my softness into submission. I understand why so many people just use tape. When I finally wear it in public—under a soft flannel shirt that is everything I want my aesthetic to be—there is no revelatory moment of clarity. Nothing is awakened. Perhaps I was too stern during those talks in the closet. Subsequent forays are similarly unremarkable, and the binder returns to its shelf.

A small part of me is disappointed. I would like an aha moment to anchor this narrative. A turning point when my body and I reach a new understanding.

Instead, it is just itchy. Perhaps this is a better metaphor.

*

Six months after I end my relationship with a cis man, my Mirena runs out and I decide to go au naturel. My GP asks about my contraceptive plan and I tell her I've given up men. She congratulates me.

It takes my period tracking app longer than my body to realise what's happening. A 27-day cycle with three days of bleeding establishes itself within eight weeks. I do not feel any more connected to my womanhood, and I don't remember tampons costing this much. Everyone tells me to use a menstrual cup instead, so I do.

I quietly add *they* to my pronouns on calls and email signatures and in introductions in queer spaces, just as an experiment. Very few people notice and most continue to use she, but when someone does try out they, I'm amazed at how good a single word can feel.

I do not talk about this to anyone.

*

Years ago, I performed in a series of nude installations about the female body created by an artist friend who'd gone on to make work about menstrual blood. I now understand her fascination with the colours and textures of our bodies, her drive to turn them into art. I, too, want to shock and provoke and celebrate, to make visible that which no one wants to see.

I've always felt more comfortable naked, even on a stage in front of strangers, than in clothing. It was nudity that got me through to the other side of disordered eating; being naked is when I feel most at home in my body. I joke that the easiest way to avoid the horrors of fashion and shopping is just to opt out, to refuse to play the game. Perhaps I am on to something there.

She has since left town—another artist priced out of the creative capital by skyrocketing rents and parasitic landlords—and moved to the South Island, where she grows vegetables in the wholesomely chaotic back yard of the house she bought with a friend. We've stayed in sporadic contact, and she invites me to her virtual fortieth birthday party. When I RSVP, I tell her I'm getting back into performing and have come out of the closet. She, too, congratulates me.

*

I fall hard for a nonbinary clown so brilliant and beautiful that I am rendered incoherently giddy the first time we kiss, and for the months to follow. They are half my size, but I find it surprisingly endearing when they borrow my clothes, their tightly muscled frame drowning in my already-oversized shirts.

There is a slight tinge of magic when our periods sync immediately, although I know intellectually this is only an accident of timing and any assertion otherwise is just a poor attempt to gloss over the fact that modern medicine regards uteri as the 'thar be dragons' section of medieval maps.

*

The first time my new co-worker, a paragon of suburban heterosexuality, asks how we met, I tell him that they directed the ballet I danced in. To his credit, he does not question that my soft body could be a ballerina. He does, however, assume they are older and male, and implies there was a hint of scandal in our courtship. He approves.

I make a mental note to lead with the fact that the ballet was called *Sapphic Lake* in future iterations of this story. It is, objectively, a cinema-worthy meet cute.

They are making a musical about gender euphoria and ask to use my flat as the venue for a festival months away. I start writing grants and fundraising for the show and then suddenly we've started an entire queer arts festival.

Fi, who has moved into my spare bedroom and continued my queer education, keeps up a steady stream of U-Haul jokes, delighting in my unabashed joy and how I blush every single time. I reassure myself I am not a lesbian stereotype because we haven't moved in together, and anyway, they aren't a woman and maybe I'm not either.

*

After a half dozen attempts on three continents, it is the thrill of queer love that finally turns me into a cyclist. I delight in meandering around on my navy men's bike with a beer crate strapped to the back. My night-time wondering changes with my wandering. The city feels different from this angle, and so does my life. It's a bit like in primary school when I left the optometrist with my new glasses and saw the individual leaves on trees for the first time.

In urban design, 'desire lines' are the paths worn by people refusing to adhere to the creative vision laid out by planners. Those swathes of dead grass that cut a hypotenuse across a corner where pedestrian after pedestrian took the shortest possible route, despite the picturesque winding path. They are used as a cautionary tale to remind planners that their work is not abstract, it will be used by real people in the course of their complex, messy lives.

On a bike, desire lines are not so much about speed as pleasure. Distance becomes secondary. I forgo efficiency and choose the long way around to avoid a messy right turn or hill. I spend more time on the waterfront, marvelling at the sea. I take the lane on busy streets, more afraid of going unnoticed than provoking a driver's rage. Taking up space makes me feel powerful.

In love, too, my desire lines have changed. I have always been physically uncomplicated, efficient, able to isolate the mechanics of pleasure from any emotional or mental complexity. Easy, in the most literal sense. I suspect this is why it took me so long to acknowledge my queerness. Now, I revel in the scenic route, savouring the sinews of their muscles in the morning light, always seeking ways to make something this beautiful last longer.

I am accused of being a tease but perhaps this is merely the natural intersection of my Taurian stubbornness and commitment to pleasure.

*

New lovers always feel like they're inventing the world, that they alone contain these multitudes. That's how we got so many goddamned poets.

Normally I process a feeling by fixating on a line or two of a song and listening to it on repeat for weeks but suddenly all the pronouns are wrong. Even Phoebe Bridgers' ethereal soprano on a cover of 'Fake Plastic Trees' —*she tastes like the real thing*—is inadequate.

English lacks imagination. Boyfriend and girlfriend are awkward enough as an adult, but what do you call the nonbinary person you've only recently started dating?

Person I'm dating is a mouthful. Lover makes people uncomfortable, which is fun but perhaps inappropriate for the office; partner feels too soon; and you can only use someone's name so many times before you sound like a sleazy salesman who's read too much Dale Carnegie.

There is so much exposition required before it's clear that I am using the singular they not to be cagey, but because it is accurate, and then what if my story has more than one character? I want to scream my queerness from the rooftops but the words just aren't cutting it.

After a few months, they tell me they love me outside the strip club in front of my apartment as their airport shuttle arrives and the point is moot. Partner will do.

*

I cannot find a hot linguistic take about how, actually, the limits of binary English are to blame for U-Haul jokes, so instead I finally read *The Argonauts* and just openly sob.

> *You ran at least a lap ahead of me, words streaming in your wake. How could I ever catch up (by which I mean, how could you want me?) … How can the words not be good enough? I want the you no one else can see, the you so close the third person need never apply.*

I become obsessed with writing in the second person, as though I am merely watching a stranger stumble towards an obvious conclusion. Sure, I cringe every time some well-meaning bartender calls us ladies, but that is only concern for the way they tense when they're misgendered, their eyes as they calculate whether it's worth saying anything. Never mind that this started before I met them and happens when I am alone.

*

Asked to describe my gender in a workshop exercise, the term *conscientious objector* pops into my head and lingers for months to follow. This is the problem with security studies. You make one joke about the constructivists and then all your metaphors are about war and suddenly you've got a crisis on your hands.

The de-securitisation literature, alas, is scant and peppered throughout with caveats that further research is needed, academic speak for 'It's definitely a problem but we have no idea how to prevent or fix it.' Classic academia—all analysis, no solutions.

Why can't I just enter 'no thank you' in the gender field of a form?

*

As spring fades into summer, we begin swimming together in the frigid sea. They dive in immediately, laughing as I yelp and slowly adjust to the cold, then bask in the sun while I swim lazy laps back and forth, peaceably alone with my body and my thoughts. For the first time since I was a kid, movement feels joyous.

My body changes, shrinks, grows firmer with a speed that is bewildering. Friends and co-workers remark that I am glowing. I marvel at sketches from a life drawing class where the contours of my deltoids are visible. I clean out my closet and give away most of the dresses.

The hills get easier. I buy a belt, then drill two, then three, then four new holes in it. All my rings are too big, so I move them to new fingers. After years of Wellington grey and black, I find myself drawn to vibrant colour. A pink acid washed denim boiler suit, orange yarn for knitting, ridiculous vintage prints from op shops. Shopping at stores I was once sized out of feels like a betrayal, but I finally understand how people could find clothing fun, affirming, even liberating.

The irony of love and acceptance accidentally changing my body after hatred failed so spectacularly is not lost on me. I don't know how to deal with the lived reality that life is definitely easier in a smaller body. I am incandescent with fury at a society that securitises our bodies into things to be controlled, hated, brutalised into submission.

*

As we stroll along Cuba Street hand-in-hand, licking ice creams, a man doubles back to shout 'unlucky, no cock for youse!' More than one leans out a car window to call me a dyke as I cycle past. A preacher at a roundabout in Auckland screeches about how homosexuals need to repent.

I should be angrier about this blatant homophobia but instead am strangely delighted. I am high on the feeling of being seen so completely, smugly satisfied that these men know I do not care whether or not they want me, and that there is nothing they can do about it. It is not unlike the old rush of going to sleep hungry, in control of something, anything, even if just my own desire.

This does not have to be a crisis. Perhaps it's an epiphany. I don't have to be a woman just because I'm shaped like one. I don't have to have an alternative to know that something no longer serves.

Was joy the key to desecuritisation all along?
Someone should tell the constructivists.

REFERENCE
You ran at least a lap … Maggie Nelson, *The Argonauts* (Graywolf Press, 2015).

SUSANNA ELLIFFE

No More Elephants

1. From the moment we are born, we are losing things.

2. We have hands that cannot grasp and legs like bowing willows. We explore the world with our tongues, each of our limbs separate from themselves, like a split-pin puzzle of parts.

3. When we drop something from sight, it is gone forever. If a person leaves the room, they are no longer ours. Everything is being lost to us, constantly, like water down a never-ending well.

4. But a few months into life, we are learning about permanence. People come back through the door and they are ours again. The blanket we drop is not lost to some great void beneath us, it is just out of sight.

5. It doesn't mean it's gone forever if it's just out of sight. That's what we learn. Yes, that's what we learn.

*

6. Elephants are highway builders. For hundreds and thousands of years they have walked the same paths with the same heavy tread. Have disappeared from view and come back again, constant as the turning world. Carved out routes for man and creature alike, linking rivers to watering holes to feeding grounds. And when elephants walk their highways, they walk atop future watering holes. Future life source. The weight of their feet makes dips in the earth like moon craters, and these dips fill with water when it rains. Tiny ecosystems are formed in their footsteps. Frogs lay eggs. Tadpoles grow. Leeches and gastropods writhe.

7. As they trample and eat and roll in the dust, elephants welcome new light into spaces. Make clearings for plants to flourish and skylights for the shrews and sengi, barely the size of their toes. Through grazing, they keep the savanna a savanna, not a forest or a tangled woodland. They clear the land, letting grasses grow for the antelopes and wildebeests. They clear the land, for the lions and hyenas to hunt for their prey uninhibited by roots or tall trees.

8. Because of this, elephants are a keystone species. Keystones are animals that define their entire ecosystem. Keystones are animals that, once gone, can make an ecosystem cease to exist altogether.

9. In this way, elephants are collectivists.

10. In this way, elephants are oblivious gods.

*

11. We hold hands as we cross the finish line, you and I. Slick in the hay-dry heat, face paint the colour of swallowtails. We fly past the sideline parents, out of breath and out of time, and we keep flying. We barrel forward with smiles on our faces, going so fast we can't stop. We're playing line-tag on the netball court, whispering secrets in our huts of pine, putting on heels for our first-ever dance, planning what jobs we want to do and where we want to go and—

12. We are on different islands. You are becoming a nurse and I am becoming transparent. I can no longer see your hand, or the finish line. But what's out of sight isn't gone forever, you see? That's what we learned, all those years ago.

13. When I see you in the supermarket, you shift before my eyes. We talk about classes and our new lives, but I can't focus on what we are. We have—both of us, inside—two tectonic plates colliding, and it makes us tremble. The gap widens, a great chasm that shifts beneath our feet.

14.   And when we part again, your hand is further than it was before. I think of a long exhale. I think of an elastic band stretching white in the middle. I think of a quote by Conan Doyle, read long ago.

15.   'We reach, we grasp, and what is left in our hands in the end? A shadow.'

*

16.   When two female elephants meet each other at a sanctuary, they wrap their trunks around one another, and glide them over the other's scars. The keepers wonder how they can be so familiar with each other, these harmless great things. But they have, in fact, met before. Twenty-three years ago, they lived together at a circus. They still remember each other's faces. The way they walk. The wrinkles in their skin.

17.   Elephants can recognise their own face, too. They stand in front of a mirror and smear at a white cross that has been painted on their head. Other animals would try to smear the glass or raise their hackles at the stranger in front of them. Would think the cross belongs to this imposter in front of them. Elephants recognise that stranger as themselves.

18.   There are only nine species in the world that have this awareness.

19.   Humans are meant to be one of them.

*

20.   She used to love the stage. Used to ascend like a rising sun and recite her lines without fear. Used to conduct choirs and write pages and pages of stories for no reason but her joy, not ever wondering what they sounded like. What they meant. What others would think of them.

21.   Now she feels a cellophane version of herself has peeled away and walked unsteadily forward from the more solid form left behind. And this 'afterward' version isn't sure how to make memories that aren't see-through. Where she doesn't say, *but remember when?*

22. And the afterward version has walked so far that she can't see the before version any more. She's just a dot in the distance. Concealed from view.

23. Something instinctual—something innate—tells her she's coming back on her own, and that she must wait for that sense of oneness to return. She's just out of sight, that's all, like a parent behind a door.

24. But when she tells a therapist she misses who she used to be, he tells her to go out and join a choir. Or a dance class. *Hell, even a bridge club!*

25. She thinks it's his way of telling her to stop waiting.

*

26. Elephants have rhythmic skin. The patterns they make in the land are mirrored in their groove-ridden hide. They live in patterns too. Move when the seasons turn dry. Follow their hallowed ground to mud-soaked places. Allow the land to regrow before they return to it, in a year or so.

27. But when they return, they're not the same place, and they're not the same routes, not any more. *How much changes in a year these days? In a month?* But they'll keep trying to walk the same way. Even if they must move in front of cars, or through resorts, or cross burning tarmac, they keep trying to walk the land they once knew. Humans shape it beyond recognition, but they look for signs that places are familiar. Not lost. Still there. Still theirs.

28. Are humans a keystone species? We are creatures that define our entire ecosystem. We are creatures that, while still living, can make that ecosystem cease to exist altogether.

29. In this way, humans are destructionists.

30. In this way, humans are oblivious gods.

*

31. The old house is made of fermented plum.

32. There's a staircase outside the colour of gargoyles. Inside it's the colour of our choosing. I pick corn-yellow. My sisters choose granny-apple green and the purple of morning clouds. On the landing, the windows are made of kaleidoscope glass. We chase one another up and down the stairs until we are out of breath. We catch colours on our skin and turn in circles till our heads spin. Make houses out of cardboard and sheets and tall-backed chairs. Let the blankets fall around us in slow motion.

33. Outside, there is an archway in the hedge. There is a dial that we turn, and the arch becomes a doorway to anywhere. We go to Sylvania and Narnia and Fairyland. When the sun streams through, the garden shifts and changes before our eyes. It is whatever we want it to be.

*

34. Elephants talk in foot-sized earthquakes. Send out their stress in seismic waves, stamp it into the bone-dry ground for miles and miles so that other herds can hear. These are the rhythms of the earth that humans aren't privy to, the ones that say, *what is happening to our land?* That say, *when will it return to how it used to be?*

35. Their tusk is like bone, but it is not bone, it is teeth, and it is not separate from the elephant. It grows in layers and layers, reaching out from the skull to the sky. It has no blood vessels, you see, so it's smooth, and its lustre improves with time. If left untouched, the tusks will grow and keep growing along with the elephant, until they are the size of small apple trees.

36. But they have not been untouched for a long while.

37. And once they are gone, they do not grow back.

*

38. Every spring, there are baby birds on the ground. They fall out of their nests and look up at the sky with great moon-struck eyes, feathers like dandelion tufts. We cup them in our hands and bring them inside. Set up a box and line it with torn tissues. Find a small dish for water and honey. Listen to them *chirp, chirp, chirp*. Dream of them growing and singing and feeding from our hands.

39. But in the morning, when we race downstairs to the box in the laundry, the linoleum is cold on our feet. Their song is empty space. An absence we have to live. Our mother says that they got stronger overnight and flew away. That they might come back and see us one day.

40. From then on, every bird we see in the sky is a bird we saved.

*

41. When an elephant dies, the herd covers them with dirt and branches and long grass. They linger near the body for days, like planets to a waning sun. And when they pass an old gravesite along their highways, they will grow quiet. They will stroke the bones with their trunks and examine the tusks and skulls, touching them lightly with their feet.

42. Twenty-four days after the death of her friend, an elephant refuses to move from its side. Everything has drooped. Her ears, her head, her trunk, every split-pin part has curved to her chest like weeping grass. She stops eating, and her skin becomes a large coat of mourning, wrinkled and dry, cracked as the mud.

43. People say that we can't call this grief. That we don't *really* know what it is elephants feel in these moments.

44. I say, surely, it's enough just to know that they do feel.

*

45. I bury the bones of my pets in the garden of the old house. Make a little wooden cross and write them poems. *To my beautiful, grey-maned cat.* She's buried in a white box beneath the dirt. Without the cross, I could not tell you where.

46. I have not revisited the old house. I think the garden will be overgrown. I think the paint will be fresh and new. I think the corn-yellow and granny-apple-green and morning clouds will be covered over with something like brown or grey. I think the old house will no longer smell of squashed plums.

*

47. I still have a photo of you and me, holding hands at that finish line, though we have not spoken in six years. I wonder at what point I can grieve something that still has a beating heart. I wonder if we have been doing that all along. I can't look at elephants now without knowing that one day these great beasts will walk full circle towards the sun, bright and blinding, and they will not walk back. We will have ivory for our metaphors and leather for our vanity. We will have patterns for our wallpapers and reconstructed skeletons. We will have *remember whens* and photographs and plastic figurines, but there will be no more elephants.

*

48. A few months into life and we are learning about permanence.

And on the pedestal, these words appear:
My name is Ozymandias, King of Kings—

49. People come back through the door and they are ours again. The blanket we drop is not lost to some great void beneath us, it is just out of sight.

Nothing beside remains. Round the decay
of that colossal Wreck, boundless and bare

50. But it doesn't mean they're gone forever if they're just out of sight. That's what we learned, isn't it? Isn't that what we learned?

The lone and level sands stretch far away.

REFERENCES

Elephants are highway builders … Don Pinnock and Colin Bell, *The Last Elephants* (Hardie Grant Books, 2019).

We reach, we grasp … Sir Arthur Conan Doyle, *The Casebook of Sherlock Holmes* [1st edn, reprinted] (J. Murray: Cape, 1974).

harmless great things … John Donne, *The Poems of John Donne* (Oxford University Press, 1966).

Elephants can recognise their own face … Frans De Waal, *Mama's Last Hug: Animal emotions and what they tell us about ourselves* (Norton, 2019).

They stand in front … Hannah Mumby, *Elephants: Birth, death and family* (William Collins, 2020).

They live a pattern too … Christen Wemmer and Catherine Christen (eds), *Elephants and Ethics: Toward a morality of coexistence* (Johns Hopkins University Press, 2008).

Elephants talk in foot-sized earthquakes … Caitlin E. O'Connell-Rodwell, 'Keeping an "ear" to the ground: Seismic communication in elephants', *Physiology* 22, 2007, pp. 287–94.

Twenty-four days after … G.A. Bradshaw, *Elephants on the Edge: What animals teach us about humanity* (Yale University Press, 2009).

And on the pedestal … Percy Bysshe Shelley, 'Ozymandias', *Selected Poems* (Oxford University Press, 1913).

BONNIE ETHERINGTON

A Fried Egg in Space

In January 2021, one day after thousands of Trump supporters stormed the US Capitol, I underwent a craniotomy far from home in Loveland, Colorado, to remove a low-grade tumour from the front left of my brain. In 2016 the World Health Organization stopped calling such tumours 'benign' as, when it comes to the brain, anything where it should not be cannot be classed as such. Generally, benign in medical terms means it is not invasive. It has not (yet) spread into healthy tissue. It is not considered immediately dangerous or harmful; if it grows, it will grow very slowly. At that point, anyway.

Most low-grade brain tumours are astrocytomas—named for the starlike cells they spring from. Astronomers and neuroscientists recently collaborated on a project where they noted the echoes in the brain of the starry structures of galaxies—or perhaps the echoes in galaxies of our brains. Our neural networks parallel the movements and networks of the universe. My tumour, however, is a cousin of the astrocytoma and has cells that look like fried eggs under a microscope, which is slightly less romantic. Such tumours make up roughly four percent of primary brain tumours diagnosed. A blurry fried egg on the MRI floating around in the galaxy of my brain, where it should not be, oozing from the grey matter into white matter. I call it Ricky. 'Tumour' makes me think of 'turmeric', which makes me think of 'Ricky'.

Names and what they hide or what they reveal are important. For example, what I have learned in my brief time living in Colorado, on the traditional lands of the Ute, Cheyenne, Arapaho and Eastern Shoshone peoples, is that terms like 'open space' or 'refuge' are often used to name areas once used for chemical waste disposal or nuclear activities. They are considered too dangerous to build housing on but 'benign' enough for recreation and animals—at least that is the going narrative. Not immediately harmful, perhaps, but what about their water contamination and the housing projects proliferating downwind? What about the cancers that sprout in their former workers, or in children who live just a little bit too close? Above it all, the Rocky Mountains rise, looking impossible to pass.

We only moved to Colorado in August 2020, just for a year so that I could take up a postdoctoral position. Due to Covid-19, we could not travel to look at any apartments before my work started and our apartment complex, dumped in the middle of farmland, seemed to be the only available option. The Rocky Flats National Wildlife Refuge is about a thirteen-minute drive over the highway from where we live. From 1952 to 1992, the Rocky Flats Plant manufactured nuclear weapons. The FBI raided the plant in 1989 after numerous environmental law violations. Since then, residents downwind of the area have consistently tried to document hazards associated with the plant. Numerous workers at the plant, as well as people living nearby, have high occurrences of brain tumours that often start out slow-growing but almost inevitably transform into high-grade, fast-growing and deadly tumours if they are allowed to progress. Meanwhile, people still hike across the Flats and ride their bikes.

My partner works at an animal care facility closer to the Flats. He and a student in my class tell me about the dogs that have steep cancer rates. A local veterinarian linked these rates to the dogs' frequent playtimes in the downwind Westminster Dog Park. Environmental officials have measured the levels of nuclear material that waft across that area and sink in its watery sites. They say it should not be enough to cause harm.

My partner and I have not lived in Colorado long enough to connect my brain tumour to the plant or to any of the other nuclear or chemical waste sites in this state. It is just bad luck (or, perhaps, good) that I have landed in an area that is very familiar with brain tumours. New Zealand is my home country but I grew up in West Papua. After my tumour was diagnosed, my family and I wracked our brains for how it came to be. I came across an article about Joe Biden's son, Beau, and his deadly glioblastoma tumour. Glioblastomas are the worst kind of brain tumour. There is no cure and they often transform from pre-existing 'benign' astrocytomas. Biden blames the US's burn pits in the Middle East for his son's tumour—places where the military burn their waste and the contaminants spread over the soldiers' clothes, skin, machines. Of course, the military's radiation use could also be a factor. I remember living on the coast in Papua, on a hill that once housed US troops during World War II, where the black smoke of American missionaries burning their rubbish in open pits spread through our house frequently. Or I think of all the times people fogged DDT to kill mosquitoes around our house and other places where we lived. My surgeon says that we will probably never know what caused this tumour—it could be caused by absolutely nothing at all, an accident of bad luck or genetics, of one cell transforming and multiplying all wrong. But, still, latching on to any potential answer offers some comfort.

When my neurologist first suggested an MRI to investigate my migraines, I thought she was overreacting and that I could not afford it, even with the relatively decent health insurance the university offered me. My partner reasoned that it was better to know than to not know and that the scan's results may put me at ease.

The MRI tube was much smaller and louder than I imagined it would be— nothing like they look on *Grey's Anatomy*. I closed my eyes and imagined that my deceased grandfather was with me. He would not mind it. The radiologist was kind, almost too kind, on my way out. I should have known something was off.

The next day I received the results in my health app. I did not comprehend them at first. I was on the phone with my mum in Nelson when I got the notification. Mum was sitting in a camp chair, watching my dad fish for trout. We were laughing about something, I can never remember what, but then I saw the results. I read them out to her: 'Most likely low-grade neoplasm? What do you think that means? What do they mean by neoplasm?' As a fairly anxiety-prone person, I have imagined encountering various illnesses over the course of my life. But never a mass in my brain.

What followed was an avalanche of tests in seven different Colorado hospitals and medical centres to rule out various diagnoses. The end result came right back to 'neoplasm': a favourite term that doctors use instead of 'tumour'. The good news, my surgeon informed me, is that low-grade means finding Ricky at this stage is almost a win. We can remove him so that he should not kill me in my forties. I am young and should heal. Once removal is achieved, I should go on with my life. Notwithstanding MRI scans every six months until something changes, until my death.

*

During our first and only summer in Colorado, the whole landscape was marked by fires. There was constant haze. One hot day in September, the sky was dark orange and ash coated our car. I went on a walk near our apartment, where there is a farm, and watched the prairie dogs huddling in their holes. In less than twelve hours the temperature plummeted and snow started to replace the ash. My supervisor taught from a hotel room as she had to evacuate from the ongoing fire. In the midst of Covid and the biggest fires in Colorado's history, the Environmental Futures class I was team-teaching seemed either too late or right on time, depending on how you looked at it. We had to conduct every class over Zoom, and our guest speakers spoke from homes as far away as Hawai'i, the UK and Canada. Once I learned about my brain tumour, I wrote my notes from the surgeon and the neurologist in the back of my class notebook. In the front were notes on visual activism for our ecologies, collaborative art practices, and multispecies relational hopes. In the back, I asked my surgeon about my risks of dying or losing critical motor and expressive functions from the craniotomy, about different tumour probabilities, prognoses and causes. I wrote notes to my partner when the online meetings triggered my migraines and nausea. I asked him for medications and ginger ale.

One of our guest speakers for the seminar was Robin Wall Kimmerer: a Potawatomi environmentalist and biologist whose book recently and belatedly exploded in popularity in the US. In her talk she spoke about being in relation with our ecosystems, including toxic places. Does anyone love those places? I wondered. How can they be in relationship with anyone or anything? Particularly, how do I be in relationship to a place like these lands in Colorado, shaped by nuclear history and fires, especially during a pandemic which seems so anti-relationship? Later I wondered if I could even be in relationship with my own body as an ecosystem when it tends to grow things like tumours in my brain. Kimmerer stated that in a toxic landscape we can 'still see resilience in the biota of these places' and can rewrite our relationships with them as we work towards something that looks like justice and healing. Hard places are places of courage, she said, and plants, despite everything, keep finding ways to grow in wounded space. They make life right where they are. Kimmerer's belief in beauty and resilience does not allow us to throw the whole place or the whole body away.

My body's tumour still feels like a dark and nasty betrayal. I wish I had been more forgiving and gentler with myself whenever I was in pain. I wish I had believed myself and not previous doctors who had simply blamed my migraines on anxiety and stress—the usual culprits when a doctor is looking at a young woman's medical records. Kimmerer's words gather in my mind. The migraines were a red flag, a call for help. They were trying to save me the whole time. My body knew and tried to let me know, too. It sent the messages its cells have access to.

*

It was deeply lonely to go through a brain tumour diagnosis in a place that seemed doubly hostile because we knew almost no one when we moved there. In the middle of a pandemic, it feels like there is no community to build on. Before Covid, a friend used to say that whenever she went somewhere with me, I would stop all the time to say hello or chat briefly with people I knew as we passed them. 'You know everyone,' she said, half frustrated, half impressed.

Upon the tumour diagnosis, my moments with medical workers did at least give me an opportunity to see someone outside my apartment. For some reason, what to wear for my doctors seemed important. I planned the outfit the night before. For MRI scans, I could not wear metal of any kind. Comfortable elastic-waisted pants and a shirt I could easily take off and replace with a gown. I chose socks with fun patterns, like bees or llamas. For trips to see my surgeon in Fort Collins, over an hour away, I chose my nicest pants that were not too constricting, so I did not have to stop often for the bathroom. At the same time, I chose clothes that felt like they allowed the surgeon to see what I am like, to see *me*. I wore my boots painted with flowers, my favourite hat. I even wore my best mask, with the black and white stripes that go with everything. As if that allowed my personality to come through. As if it would ensure that, in the surgery, I would live.

Before the surgery, I had a functional MRI scan in Colorado's largest hospital. The functional MRI provides more information than a regular MRI. It maps out the essential areas of certain parts of the brain. I did this so my surgeon knew where to cut in order to avoid any speech areas. Surgeons and radiologists call these areas of the brain that allow us to use language, or to move, or enable other sensory areas, the 'eloquent' areas. They allow us to process information and express ourselves.

My partner, as for all my scans, could only drop me off in the carpark and wait outside. But even if someone can come into the waiting room with you, as in pre-Covid times, the MRI is still isolating.

For this scan, I had to think of common nouns beginning with certain letters or complete easy sentences. The first letter was 'A'. All I could think of was 'asshole'. I wanted to be creative afterwards, to make up for it, but it is hard to feel creative inside a large noise-filled machine, even though the technicians had gently covered me with a warm steamed blanket. I did not feel so 'eloquent'.

It did not matter, though. Afterwards, the scan showed my brain all lit up in rainbows: simple words had bloomed great arcs of colour.

Kimmerer suggested in her talk that we should not privilege vision or language when we are trying to pay attention with compassion to the landscapes around us. Language, especially, can be a barrier to perception. It can facilitate understanding, but it also has the power to raise hurdles, blocks and gaps. So, Kimmerer asked her audience to try to cultivate a languageless way of knowing, which might be exhausting but also rewarding. As I listened to her, I wondered if I could also apply this thinking to the landscape of my brain, of my body. I always thought language was where I was most powerful, where I had the most strength, where I had the ability to make relations.

But my tumour was nestled so close to my speech areas. After the cranio-tomy, my surgeon said, I could have speech delays for a short time. Especially when naming things. In the end, though, I signed the consent forms.

*

Against all odds, my mother managed to fly to the US from New Zealand, changing her flights to arrive just before my surgery after it was bumped up. Mum was not used to all the mask-wearing or having to find empty corners in the airport to eat and drink. 'Remember to wipe down your bags with sanitising wipes,' I told her. And then told her again and again. When she arrived, we did not hug until she had quarantined her belongings in an empty closet and until after she had showered. If the timing had not been so urgent, she would have quarantined herself, but this time we trusted she had made it virus-free.

Of course, she could not visit me in the hospital, which was located one hour north of our home. The night before the surgery, I cried next to her, feeling like my body and everything else was running so swiftly out of time.

My dad called me in the middle of the New Zealand night as we drove to the hospital in the early hours. He prayed and it left me some peace while the leftover Christmas lights in front of the hospital glowed blue. In mid-winter, the sun had not started to rise for us.

In the preoperative room, as a nurse inserted needles into my hands, attached a patch to my lower back to prevent bedsores and took my temperature, I asked her if this hospital had seen many brain tumours. 'We never used to,' she said. 'But in the last ten years, many.'

Before my craniotomy, my surgeon warned that if any residual tumour was left over, or if it was not what she expected, then radiotherapy and chemotherapy would be on the table. I am a researcher whose work focuses, in part, on literature that documents and protests the devastating effects of irradiation from nuclear testing in the Pacific. And now, also living on lands so close to a former nuclear facility in Colorado, the irony of this position—of potentially needing radiation to save my brain—did not escape me.

When it was time for the surgery, I said goodbye to my partner. His eyes above his mask—he wore his best mask, too—held mine.

Sometimes fear is white hot. Sometimes it is a puff of cold air that dissipates with someone's joke or touch. Sometimes it is straps around my heart and throat, pulling tight. Sometimes it is a flash, a cry in the night.

*

According to Celtic mythology, there are places in nature that are 'thin': that is, they are places where we suddenly might find ourselves not far from the spirits and their world. Waking up from the surgery also felt like being in a thin place.

I reached to feel the bandage on my head, so I knew the surgery was real. A nurse checked my monitors. She asked me questions. I could understand her and that gave me relief. I answered yes or no, but nothing more. I was tired. After checking on the monitors, my nurse discussed her weekend plans with one of the assistants. I slept and woke, slept and woke.

*

Much to my partner's distress, I spent much more time in recovery than he expected. Finally, at seven o'clock that first night, the nurses wheeled me into the high-dependency surgical unit where he was waiting. I still was not very interested in words. But I could thank the nurses, ask how Josh was.

I was grateful that I still felt like *me*. Allowing someone to go into my brain and remove a piece felt like a dark threat to my whole sense of self. I was thankful to realise that I still knew things, could understand things. I could speak sentences.

Names were harder, though. I knew exactly what I was trying to name. I knew how the name's shape ballooned in my head. But it would not come out. I wanted to ask my partner about his Pokémon game. I could only think of the word 'porcupine'. I wanted to say the word 'vase', or 'bagel', the name of a newish friend, or the name of the show my mother liked to watch (*Home Town*). The names would not come to me, especially words I learned more recently. Later I saw the notes from my speech therapist, who I only vaguely remembered from the day after surgery. She wrote that I underscored across the board for complex thoughts and expressions, though she also blamed this on extreme fatigue.

Names were important. But I did not know about my therapist's notes at that time, and I was too tired to struggle over word specifics. I knew that I still knew things. I knew that I could understand the world, with or without words, and also that I needed rest.

After I was discharged from the hospital, my mum and I watched medical shows on TV, and I saw how patients' family members all crowded into the room during major diagnoses. I knew my grief at losing that, due to Covid, but also knew how hard it was to acknowledge that kind of grief in the US, where there are so many unacknowledged layers of grief in its history, including all the different types of loss, big and small, regarding what the virus has taken or forced some of us to reckon with. I remembered my rage every time an anti-masker said that anyone who died from Covid had pre-existing conditions, not realising that they probably also had pre-existing conditions, and knowing that if I, at thirty-one, died from Covid they would blame it on my brain tumour, that my death would be irrelevant.

But I grew in strength; my mother took me for walks. First for five minutes, then ten, then more. I was unsteady on my feet, but what I loved most was a walk to see the prairie dogs and the horses over the railroad tracks behind our apartment complex. One day we saw a coyote. There were two nesting bald eagles in the distance. Before this year, I never thought I could see bald eagles on a daily walk. It was very cold. It kept snowing but we looked out for early buds on the trees. Several months earlier, I had seen hundreds of geese swooping towards a small lake in the distance—their resting place on their way south. My partner told me of the owl he heard calling from the parking garage.

My words started to come back, but I took comfort that I could still understand the world without them and know that there are other kinds of knowing, too. Kimmerer, of course, is not hostile to words. She writes that names help us shape the world, just like other forms of knowing, and allow us to become reacquainted with it, too. But having that space away from names allowed me to reckon with the vulnerability of the body and to face the fragility of lands where colonial powers refuse to acknowledge lasting, meaningful responsibilities, accountabilities.

When I received the pathology report for my tumour, I had a new name to understand what was going on in my brain. I choose to keep this name to myself for now, but those of you with any familiarity with brain tumours probably already know it. Naturally, I googled that name immediately, found out that some pathologists see the cells of that tumour as fried eggs nestled within brain cells, whereas others envision it as octopus-like, with tentacles infiltrating. But as I learned more about this tumour, I felt I knew it already. Like I have always known it.

Perhaps the fried egg in my brain has not been an anomaly for me for some time, much like how the satellites that now wheel above us in the atmosphere are no longer strangers to space. As I write this, NASA just flew a helicopter on Mars. We are a part of the earth's ecosystems and even space's ecosystems. We have added to, subtracted from, and exponentially multiplied our impacts on those ecosystems, and they affect us in good ways and desperately difficult ways. Our actions led to Covid's proliferation throughout the world, and now they affect our own proliferation, too. We are part of the earth's biota, as is the tumour in my head. It grew from a distortion in my cells. We have to live with these things, sometimes die with these things. The tumour is trying to make its way and I must negotiate my own world around it, make peace with my body that grows it, work to live through its impacts as much as possible. All of us, human and non-human, body and cell, are figuring out practices of living and relationship on deeply damaged lands as we spin in one tiny part of a still mostly unknown universe.

This essay was previously published in Overland *issue 249 (Summer 2022): https://overland.org.au/previous-issues/issue-249/feature-a-fried-egg-in-space/*

REFERENCE

One of our guest speakers … Robin Wall Kimmerer, *Braiding Sweetgrass: Indigenous wisdom, scientific knowledge, and the teaching of plants* (Milkweed Editions, 2013).

NORMAN P. FRANKE

'Dreams of Birds …'

The New Zealand father-in-law of one of my former students was imprisoned
in the Stalag VIII-A in Germany. After the war, the English-speaking prisoners
published an illustrated book about their time in the camp.[1] The student
intended to write a research essay about the commemorative book and wanted
to include his father-in-law's personal memories. The life of the English-
and French-speaking prisoners of Stalag VIII-A was often tough and full of
privation, but they had considerable privileges compared to the Polish and
Russian prisoners. On Sunday afternoons, the English-speaking POWs could
play music or football. They performed Shakespeare plays; black-and-white
images of the memory book show a male Lady Macbeth, wrapped in an old
curtain, declaiming verses on an improvised stage, probably part of a former
inn near Görlitz/Zgorzelec.

The student and I started to translate parts of the memorabilia into German
in order to send them along with our research findings to the Stalag Museum,
which was erected after the war on the grounds of the former POW camp. Run
jointly by Poles and Germans, the museum aims at being not only a historical
memorial but also a modern meeting place for young people, peace researchers
and artists.[2]

During our research into Stalag VIII-A, we discovered that Olivier
Messiaen's groundbreaking piece of modern classical music, 'Quatuor pour la
Fin de Temps' ('Quartet for the End of Time'), had been premiered at Stalag
VIII-A. It is quite possible, even likely, that the student's father-in-law was
among the audience. Messiaen had composed the music in the camp; a music-
loving German guard, Carl-Albert Brüll, had organised notebooks with staves
and isolated rooms for the French composer, who was taken prisoner in 1940
off Verdun.

The student and I were in the middle of researching and translating when, against significant protests from students and the community, the new managers of the School of Humanities at the University of Waikato decided to close the German department. We could not finish our envisaged research and translation collaboration with the museum in Görlitz/Zgorzelec. Meanwhile, I had started writing a portrait poem about Messiaen. This, too, remained unfinished.

Years later, I was listening to a live performance of Messiaen's 'Quatuor' by the fantastic New Zealand Trio. One of the musicians, the clarinetist Jonathan Cohen, spoke a few introductory words and pointed out the unusual conditions in which the work was created. In addition to the unique circumstances of the composition's origins, Jonathan Cohen also mentioned the disputed number of the reported premiere listeners, which ranges from a few hundred to a few thousand (more about this below). Listening to the quartet again inspired me to resume the writing of my poem on Messiaen. I wrote in my room behind the garage, listening on the old CD system to further works by the composer.

For Olivier Messiaen

Les rêves d'oiseaux sont Träume der Vögel
sind les rêves de l'amour terrestre de Dieu; dreams
of birds are dreams of God's earthly love.

Pre-surgically, your picture began to fade from your wife's mind, for ever
her memories, your gaze—shining summer meadows in the Bois du
                                                            Boulogne;
the morning concert of sparrows, black bird, Löweneckerchen, de l'aluette,
                                                            monk
warbler; those nights together in the cafés of the Rue du Martyrs,

20 meters above floor level at the keys of the Cavaillé-Coll organ
where she had written and turned you scores; and you played
with the morning stars and let the suffering servant sing
that He will witness at the last upon the dust.

I mohio ano ia ki te reo o nga manu, e kii ana te hoia

At Stalag VIII-A they gave you a personal guard and locked you up,
near the commander's office or in the latrine block, so you could compose
in peace

Quatuor pour la fin du temps.

Four hundred (four thousand), prisoners and guards heard the Angel of the
                                                                        Apocalypse
stop the continuum of time on an out of tune piano; stop European
music, the long-vexed soul, crushing words. Memories of the beloved
and her nurse's hungry eyes, burnt Logos turned
flesh: The Seventh Trumpet.

Paper with staves an art-loving officer slipped you, official stamps showing
Aquila chrysaetos; carved from sliced winter potatoes: your dismissal

back into posthistoire, the grand city of Paris; unearthly sounds
of *Turangalîla*, the morning concert of sparrows, skylarks, de l'aluette,
monk warblers, morning meadows in the Bois du Boulogne

and the ever-faithful song
the oblivious nightingale sings.

During the research process of the poem, I stumbled time and again over
an astonishing wealth of scholarly, socio-historical but even scientific 'chance
poetry': atmospheric, aesthetic and intellectual words and text passages, which,
for the purpose of these explorations, I would like to call 'research poetry' or
'lyrical research' and which I will try to point out and interpret.

Olivier Messiaen (1908–1992) was a composer, organist and ornithologist
and is considered one of the masters and innovators of modern classical
music. In his music, he processed influences from Gregorian chant, French
and German organ traditions, the troubadours, East Asian musical and literary

ideas and motifs (e.g. Javanese tonality and instruments, haiku) and natural sounds—especially birdsong. Messiaen also took a special interest in musical number symbolism and Catholic theology and mysticism.

I originally encountered Messiaen's music as a student in the rather chilly Marienkirche (St Mary's Church) in Lübeck.[3] Since the Marienkirche is located only a few kilometres from the Baltic Sea, is built as a brick basilica modelled on the Soissons Cathedral scheme and is almost forty metres high in the central nave, it is difficult to heat. I listened intently, slightly frozen but completely fascinated, to some movements from Messiaen's 'La Nativité du Seigneur: Neuf méditations pour orgue'. I have been a fan of his music ever since.

The core and starting point of my Messiaen portrait poem is the first stanza about the dreams of birds. It is entwined in three languages and thus refers to three important European music and linguistic traditions that had an impact on Messiaen. The trilingual opening lines also refer to the absurd tragedy of the world wars of the twentieth century. In all three languages (German, French and English), the term 'dreams of birds' (in double genitive) has at least a double meaning due to its complex semantics: the birds dream, or they are dreamed. The latter points in the direction of Freud's and Jung's dream interpretation, the former in the direction of Messiaen's mysticism of love.

Messiaen incorporated the melody, harmony and rhythm of bird calls into a number of his compositions (including 'Catalog d'Oiseaux', 'La Fauvette des Jardins', 'Petites Esquisses d'Oiseaux' and 'Le Merle Noir'). The opening passage of my poem may have formed under the unconscious impression of the fourth movement of Messiaen's *Turangalîla Symphony* ('Jardin du Sommeil d'Amour'). But it emerged especially in the wake of Messiaen's 'Réveil des Oiseaux' ('Awakening of the Birds'), which made me think about the sleep— and dreams—of birds.[4] 'Réveil des Oiseaux' is dedicated to the memory of the ornithologist Jacques Delamain. It premiered on 11 October 1953 at the Donaueschingen Festival with the Baden-Baden Südwestfunk orchestra playing. Yvonne Loriod, Messiaen's second wife, was the soloist.

Messiaen's work found multiple resonances in New Zealand and helped establish a decolonial New Zealand musical tradition.[5] Examples are the work of composers Robin Maconie, who attended one of Messiaen's master classes at the Paris Conservatoire in 1963–64, and Jenny McLeod, whom Messiaen met a year later. Conversely, New Zealand music also influenced Messiaen. Maconie sent Messiaen vinyl recordings of New Zealand birdsong; the songs of bellbird and tūī were subsequently heard in Messiaen's musical vision of the Heavenly Jerusalem, 'Couleurs de la Cité Céleste' (1964); and the songs of tūī and kākāpō—mediated through recordings by Jenny McLeod and Nicholas Armfelt—in Messiaen's last work 'Concert à Quatre' (1991).[6]

In 2017, Hamilton-based composer Martin Lodge created and directed a musical and narrative performance under the title 'Manu Kaewa' ('Wild Birds'), which, in addition to drawing on ideas of Messiaen's bird compositions, takes up the rich musical reception of ornithological sounds in the Māori tradition. Large passages of the works are based on Jackie Tuaupiki's poetry, in which he develops a unique holistic metaphysics of birdsong from a mātauranga Māori perspective. Stressing the interrelationship of all animate and inanimate beings, and a universalist ecological ontology, one of Tuaupiki's poems about water and birds reads:

> Korokī, korohī, korokoro tūī, tūī, tūī, tuitaia te muka onomata / kiwi, weka, kuaka, kōkako, kū, kū, kererū / ore te koera, ka ngahae te rangi hei tiu rangitāmirotia ngā rire hau (My call, your call, the tūī bird sings, unite the ancestral rule / oh, humanity, kiwi, weka, kuaka, kōkako and kererū / shine through a superior understanding of nature).[7]

In recent years, the 'naturalist Messiaen' has been stressed by scholars, but although Messiaen was able to identify more than 700 bird calls and took part in early ecology debates, it seems to me that the 'scientific' dimension of Messiaen can easily be overstated.[8] In Messiaen's opera about Francis of Assisi, the saint who understood the language of birds, *Saint François d'Assise*, it is obvious that Messiaen considered birds to be more than the feathered evolutionary descendants of airborne dinosaurs. Rather, they were ancient creatures defying gravity, and seen in a completely different, metaphysical, light. In the wake of the composer's interpretation of the Book of Genesis, and its elaborations by Thomas Merton, Romano Guardini and Hans Urs von Balthasar, birds were understood as witnesses and harbingers of a creatio continua (continuous creation), a complex and beautiful natural world that was part of a continuing divinatory project. Current Messiaen scholarship also discusses the potential influence of Teilhard de Chardin's creation theology on

Messiaen's music.[9] For Messiaen, the feathered creatures were distantly related to those other feathered beings in the biblical tradition, the angels (from the Greek ἄγγελος, 'messengers'). Like the divine messengers, the birds—even the most inconspicuous, who are often the most musically gifted, such as the nightingale and blackcap—were messengers of a divine scheme of beautiful and harmonious creation. Martin Lodge reminds us that many of Messiaen's greatest works 'combine visionary Christian mysticism with the songs of birds, whom Messiaen regarded as superlative and divinely created.'[10] Written in the Görlitzer Stalag, 'Quatuor pour la Fin de Temps' shows a pronounced musico-theological emphasis on the apocalypse (further considerations on this later). Messiaen's ornithological views include aspects of Pauline creation theology, which sees the entire creation in need of redemption but also already allows a glimpse of divine harmony and love, which Messiaen wants to celebrate as an avowed 'musicien de joi'.[11]

Claire Delbos, Messiaen's first wife, suffered from memory loss, possibly after an overdose of pre-surgical anaesthetics. My portrait poem lists the birds that particularly inspired Messiaen in his musical oeuvre and which his wife would never remember again. Delbos was a talented composer and musician herself. Compositions by Messiaen such as 'Poèmes pour Mi' ('Mi' was Delbos's nickname) are dedicated to her. The 'Poèmes' set Messiaen's own libretto to music. The libretto is a weird and wonderful love poem, a 'surrealist mixture' of passages of the biblical 'Song of Songs', its church adaptations, Catholic hymns and lyrical celebrations of the landscape around the old Château Saint-Benoît in Auvergne, their retreat and love nest. Delbos probably endured fifteen years of massive or complete dementia before she died.[12] A deeply devout Catholic, Messiaen did not enter into a new relationship through all those years, despite having fallen in love with a woman called Yvonne Loriod. The two longed for closeness, and Messiaen wrote practically all of his later piano oeuvre for her.[13] He married Loriod in 1961, two years after Claire Delbos's death.[14] Georg Predota called the tragedy and musical sublimation of Messiaen's love for Loriod 'Love on a Cosmic Scale'—pure research poetry, that.[15]

I composed English, German and French versions of my poem, 'For Olivier Messiaen'. In the English and French versions, the word 'Löweneckerchen' sticks out among the names of the forgotten birds. It is a Westphalian dialectal compound that stands for the skylark (*Alauda arvensis*; French, alouette) and at the same time provided the title of one of the Grimm brothers' best-known fairy tales: 'Das Singende, Springende Löweneckerchen' ('The Singing, Springing Lark').[16] Larks play a special role in Messiaen's work.[17] The beautiful French, perhaps originally Canadian-French, folk song 'Alouette, Gentille Alouette' is also known in Anglo-Saxon countries and in Germany. When I looked for a Messiaen connection, I couldn't find any. And yet this reencounter with the tragicomic song was an important addition to my 'research lyrics' because it playfully describes the destruction of this grandiose singer by time and fate ('Alouette, je te plumerai': 'Skylark, I will pluck you'), alouette being the traditional symbol of morning love. In my further research on this bird, I came across the following passage of a kind of 'taxonomic research poetry':

> *The bird literally climbs up on its song. In doing so, it climbs incessantly trilling in a spiral flight to heights between 50 and 100 meters, remains in the air for a long time and then suddenly nosedives down again, the last part with its wings folded. During the dive, the lark does not interrupt her singing for a moment. Just above the ground, the bird unfolds its wings and swings up again.*[18]

I drew a line from Messiaen's own 'fairy tale mysticism '('The greatest impression I received came from my mother […]; All this time of my youth […] my mother raised me in a climate of poetry and fairy tales, which, regardless of my vocation as a musician, was the origin of everything I did later'[19]—sheer research poetry) to the seminal story by the Grimm Brothers. The Löweneckerchen is a type of fairy tale that combines various archetypal characters and narrative types. Thus, it corresponds to, among other things, the fairy tale typology of Mary Louise von Franz. With a request to the reader to hear the following terms with their research-lyrical ears: 'Annunciation of a promised child', 'The quest', 'The fight with the dragon', 'The purchased wedding night', 'Marriage to the beast' (as in the French fairy tale 'Beauty and the Beast').[20]

It is particularly noteworthy that in the 'Singing, Springing Lark' the woman is the heroine and, unlike in almost all western heroic myths from Homer to Hollywood, she liberates the man, and not the other way around. This archetypical tale is not least the basis of Hans Christian Andersen's romantic tale 'The Little Mermaid', which the Danish poet provided with an unhappy ending, unlike in the Grimm version.

The moving poetry of the courageous and patient woman, who does not ask her father to bring her gold and diamonds, as her older sisters do, but asks for the living joy and song of the lark instead, and who saves her man in great danger, is summarised in this passage—an unparalleled research lyric find:

> I followed you for seven years, I was with the sun and moon and with the four winds and asked about you and I helped you against the dragon; do you want to forget me completely? But the prince slept so hard that it just seemed to him as if the wind was rustling in the pine trees outside.[21]

It was women, Messiaen's mother, Cécile Sauvage, and both of his wives, who saved the always somewhat unworldly and sometimes clumsy Messiaen from the dragons of the modern age.

There are many lark habitats near Stalag VIII-A, in which jubilant skylarks 'climb up on their song'. From anecdotal reports, I had learned that Māori POWs paid special attention to the birds of the region because, in Māori tradition, the birds have always been regarded as universal symbols of freedom, mediators of omens and messengers of the gods. At the beginning of his first stay in Germany, when he attended a conference on Commonwealth literature in Kiel (1982), Hone Tuwhare spoke only a little German, so initially he conversed with the birds of the Baltic city. He laid down his thoughts on the natural and universal language of birds in the poem 'Für Mich der Vogel Schön Singst'.[22] The German title of the piece translates roughly into 'The bird sings beautifully for me'. It was the recollection of Hone Tuwhare's bird poem that inspired the portrait poem's passage of a Māori soldier professing the creator's knowledge of bird language in te reo. According to Richard Nilsen,

> [the camp's] prisoners and officers [witnessed] … the quartet begin with a clarinet playing the same notes a blackbird sings. The answer came from a violin imitating a nightingale. Meanwhile a piano and cello created the harmonic nimbus that sits as still as the surface of a windless pond.[23]

The poetic vision of the Angel of the Apocalypse who stopped time at the premiere in Stalag VIII-A on an out-of-tune piano appeared in the wake of an oral report by a former POW and the memories of Messiaen. I emphasised the apocalyptic aspect of Messiaen's music; on listening to Quatuor, the musicians of the premiere and many of the first listeners also experienced a strong liberating effect. But how many listeners were actually there at the premiere? Hundreds might have fitted with difficulty into the camp's barrack-turned-concert-hall, Baracke 27-B. But thousands, as Messiaen suggests in his memories? Can both be right at the same time? Recent research considers thousands of listeners to be far exaggerated.[24] I think, however, as paradoxical as it sounds, both are true: there must have been a few hundred prisoners, mostly English- and French-speaking, in camp barrack 27-B, but thousands more, Russian and Polish POWs, were listening in front of the doors and in the far-off camp barracks. It seems to me that there are research-lyric findings that may have the potential to challenge the binary logic of exclusivity (apocalypse or freedom, hundreds or thousands of listeners).

In the late twentieth century, European theological thinkers in the Judeo-Christian tradition repeatedly asked themselves why an omnipotent god did not end the world after the mass murders of the twentieth century—after two world wars, after Auschwitz and Hiroshima. Why was the experiment of human history, this experimentum mundi, 'red in tooth and claw' not cancelled? Was this god not present in history—was he dead? Did he perhaps die with the murdered victims and the mutually killing perpetrators, into whose life and free will he had laid his fate? Wasn't he all-powerful and benevolent after all? Had he lost his memory? Had he never existed? But wasn't the meaning of history, then, placed even more in the hands of finite and fallible Higher Primates? Reading European literature and listening to European music, I have often asked myself these questions. What theologians' doxology cannot conclusively explain, some artists of the twentieth century tried to express and to emulate in their works.

One of them, Olivier Messiaen, stopped time in January 1941 in 'Quatuor pour la Fin du Temps' and declared the European experiment of civilisation, the eschatology of power and 'progress', to have failed. Almost one year later to the day, in January 1942, the 'Wannsee Conference' took place, not far from Görlitz, at which high-ranking Nazi officials decided over breakfast that the 'final solution to the Jewish question' was through industrial extermination camps. It had been advocated by fanatic ideologues, including academics and artists, who demanded the persecution of minorities. Jews, Roma and Sinti, the disabled and political opponents who were regarded as enemies of the state. Messiaen understood the European civil wars, the atrocities of the twentieth century and the end of political eschatology and historicity not only as consequences of ideological or political aberrations but as the result of a profound spiritual crisis. Paul Crossley, who knew the composer well, submitted: 'He regarded modern society with complete horror—he thought that it lacked any kind of spiritual dimension whatsoever.'[25]

When time and history end (in music), but chronology still ticks on, posthistoire arises. Perhaps 'post-history' can be dated from a day in January in the early 1940s. Postmodernism, then, is not just an intellectual and socio-historical paradigm shift towards deontology and a new perspectivism (which, incidentally, was ideologically prefigured by the reactionary Nietzsche,[26] who supplied key concepts of many fascist discourses) but the aftermath, perhaps the 'satyr's game', of a failed modernity whose best intellectual and spiritual traditions—Enlightenment and Human Rights, universality based on Judeo-Christian traditions, as well as social justice and the ecology of creation—could not prevail over colonialist, fascist and exploitative capitalist/neoliberal powers.

After Messiaen's return from the camp to Paris—some say with a fake stamp carved from winter potatoes—life remained somewhat mundane. Messiaen's was an exemplary grotesque return into postmodern chronological time. The composer preceded the experience of many intellectuals born after the war, into postmodernism. After all the destruction, life and love, strangely, continued. The birds were still singing. After all the suffering, did history, including European history, get a second (divine) chance?[27] Was history to be understood as a great game, perhaps meaningless, but not senseless, forever continuing, even repeating—a game in time, like music?

In 1946, Messiaen was commissioned by Serge Alexandrovich Koussevitzky to write a large orchestral work for the Boston Symphony Orchestra: the *Turangalîla Symphony*. It was a time when Messiaen also studied the forbidden love of Tristan and Isolde of Celtic mythology as well as mystical theology and theories about Ludic cosmology. Inspired by the Indian music theorist Sarangadeva, in whom he found the rhythmic structure of the deçi tala, and the Sanskrit title, and probably also inspired by the discursive history of Dante (commedia divina) and the medieval mystic Henricus Suso, the 'troubadour of divine love', who understood the world and Being as a divine game, love at its core, but ever endangered (ludus amoris), the *Turangalîla Symphony* emerged. As Messiaen submitted:

'Lîla' literally means play—but play in the sense of the divine action upon the cosmos, the play of creation, destruction, reconstruction, the play of life and death. 'Lîla' is also love. 'Turanga': this is the time that runs, like a galloping horse; this is time that flows, like sand in an hourglass. 'Turanga' is movement and rhythm. 'Turangalîla' therefore means all at once love song, hymn to joy, time, movement, rhythm, life and death.[28]

Since Plato, Western, European philosophy has been mainly based on eidetic premises, especially in its conceptual work. This extends far into the area of systematic theology, which is heavily influenced by Neoplatonism. God and the world, history, eschatology and theodicy have been viewed and conceptualised from an imaginary 'eye of God' perspective, from a detached, idealised 'bird's eye view'. In Messiaen's and von Balthasar's oeuvre, but also in non-European locations, in Lodge's and Tuaupiki's Māori universalism, the acoustic sense is increasingly rehabilitated—in analogy to the calling and concerts of birds. What emerges are new epistemological, but also musico-theological paradigms. Sound and rhythm become metaphors—and manifestations—of truths about the world and human life. In contrast to, for example, the progressive Nietzsche, who, despite being one of the pioneers of a new philosophy of the body, the senses and particularly hearing, would only ever speak and sing and hope for an echo in privileged individuals (exemplified in *Thus Spoke Zarathustra*),[29] Messiaen, Lodge and von Balthasar emphasise sonority, symphonic teamwork, democratic resonance. As von Balthasar submits: 'Truth is symphonic',[30] and Messiaen puts it lyrically:

A true music, that is to say, spiritual, a music which may be an act of faith; a music which may touch upon all subjects without ceasing to touch upon God; an original music … whose language may open a few doors, take down some yet distant stars.[31]

If there are still doors leading to truth and transcendence, they are most likely symphonic, and, through Messiaen, also synaesthetic-symphonic, probably less so in the sense of classical symphonies, probably less harmonic and more rhythmically complex—symphonies of symphonies perhaps. Collections of amazing flashes of beauty and knowledge—just like in research poetics—a fugal stretto of metaphysical moments behind the world of an antipodean garage.

REFERENCES

1   The book *Interlude, Prisoners of War in Stalag VIII-A in Gorlitz, Lower Silesia, Germany* (Partridge and Cooper, 1945) is primarily about British prisoners. *Prisoners of War* by W. Wynne Mason (War History Branch, Dept of Internal Affairs, 1954) is a factual overview of the situation of New Zealand POWs in particular but offers little personal insight into their situation.

2   https://www.meetingpoint-music-messiaen.net/about-stalag-viii-a/ 'The role of the Center is not only to be a memorial place, but to give room for development and a broad range of artistic activities and creative development.'

3   It is the church to which the young Johann Sebastian Bach travelled in the autumn of 1705, hiking 450km on foot to hear the old Danish organ master Dietrich Buxtehude and to apply for this lucrative organist position. The condition was to marry Buxtehude's daughter as well. But Bach was probably already in love with his distant relative Maria Barbara, with whom he entered into a marriage two years later when he had a better position and with whom he eventually had seven children—see the book by the English music historian Horatio Clare, *Something Of His Art: Walking to Lübeck with J.S. Bach* (Little Toller, 2018) and the corresponding radio broadcast, 'Research lyrics', in the BBC3 *Slow Radio* series (12/2017). The Marienkirche in Lübeck continues the Pre-Christmas Concerts from the time of Buxtehude to this day; French Late Romanticism and Modernism are very often brought to the fore in the organ recitals. Incidentally, Bach and Messiaen shared a strong interest in the biblical 'Song of Songs' and the idea that erotic love and religious and musical mysticism could be related.

4   Realistically and scientifically, do birds dream? And if so, of what? Some scientific insights are perplexing—e.g. 'What do birds dream about? Singing, researchers suggest.' Perhaps they are dreaming with their 'robustus archistratalis', an archaic cerebral singing and memory centre of the brain: 'research poetry'! https://www.chicagotribune.com/news/ct-xpm-1998-12-17-9812180355-story.html

5   Martin Lodge, 'The French influence on New Zealand Music', in *La Nouvelle-Zélande et La France*, Martin Piquet & Francine Tolron (eds) (Université Paris Dauphine, 2006), p. 133. Among the international organists interpreting Messiaen, Christopher Hainsworth, who was born in Wellington, deserves special mention.

6   Ibid. Messian was fascinated by the fact that before the arrival of humans and their domestic animals, Aotearoa was essentially a land of birds.

7   From the poem 'Wai Rere, Wai Tuhi, Puna Wai Tea.' The libretti of 'Manu Kaewa' were kindly made available to me by Martin Lodge, to whom I am also deeply indebted for other important information—and research poetry—concerning this essay.

8   See also David Kraft, *Birdsong in the Music of Olivier Messiaen* (CreateSpace, 2013).

9   Galina Ye Kaloshina, 'Theological concepts in the work of Olivier Messiaen', *Music Scholarship/Problemy Muzykal'noj Nauki* 9 (2), 2011, pp. 92–97.

10 Martin Lodge, 'Put to music by Messiaen', in *French Footprints on New Zealand Soil* (French Embassy to New Zealand, 2009), p. 76.

11 'Because the creature itself also shall be delivered from the bondage of corruption into the glorious liberty of the children of God. For we know that the whole creation groaneth and travaileth in pain together until now.' Rom. 8. 21, 22—both as a theological and poetic thought, realised in typical Pauline rhythmical prose: pure research poetry. (cf. Messiaen's reevaluation of musical rhythms). See also Siglind Bruhn, 'Religious symbolism in the music of Olivier Messiaen', *The American Journal of Semiotics* 13 (1), pp. 277–309.

12 The research literature is not always clear about the progression of her disease and her memory loss. My poem's semantics ('Pre-surgically, your picture began to fade from your wife's mind') tries to avoid anachronism.

13 https://www.umpgclassical.com/en-GB/News/2014/12/Messiaen-Poemes-pour-Mi.aspx

14 When I was thinking about Messiaen's work and his love relations, it seemed to me that there was a parallel to the theologian Dietrich Bonhoeffer: War and fate forced both Messiaen and Bonhoeffer to renounce erotic love, and both created grandiose works of love. Both can be viewed as deprived modern saints whose life and work in those often vulgar, materialistic and frivolous times of (post-) modernity seem particularly peculiar and brave.

15 https://interlude.hk/love-cosmic-scale-olivier-messiaen-claire-delbos-yyonne-loriod/

16 The fairy tale's title can be literally translated as 'The singing, springing Lion-Lark'. Löwen-Eckerchen is a compound of 'Löwe' (lion) and 'Eckerchen' (in standard German meaning 'squirrel' or 'acorn', 'beechnut', but in Westphalia also 'lark'). *The Lady and the Lion* is a frequently used English title. Grimm Brüder, *Kinder- und Hausmärchen. Vollständige Ausgabe* (Artemis & Winkler, 1999) pp. 437–43.

17 See also Roderick Chadwick and Peter Hill, *Olivier Messiaen's* Catalog D'oiseaux: *From conception to performance* (Cambridge University Press, 2018), p. 96ff. And also Messiaen's *Musical Creed*, cf. *Melos* 12, 1985, p. 384.

18 Collective of authors, 'Vögel der Felder, Wiesen und Moore', in *Vögel unserer Region* (Atlas Verlag, 2000).

19 Claude Samuel, *Entretiens avec Olivier Messiaen* (Pierre Belfond, 1986), p. 12.

20 In addition, there are a number of magical objects of great archetypical and poetic significance: the nut, the griffin, the egg, the night-wind. A long-term friend of the Nobel Prize laureate (Physics) Wolfgang Pauli, Marie Louise von Franz was one of the most renowned Jungian analysts and interpreters of European fairy tales.

21 Grimm Brüder, *Kinder- und Hausmärchen*. p. 442.

22 Hone Tuwhare, *Deep River Talk. Collected Poems* (University of Hawai'i Press, 1994), p. 156. Although grammatically unconventional, Tuwhare's creative title highlights the notion of the bird as an interlocutor, a 'you'.

23 Messiaen relates: 'Between three and four in the morning, the awakening of birds: a solo blackbird or nightingale improvises surrounded by a shimmer of sound, by a halo of trills lost very high in the trees. Transpose this onto a religious plane and you have the harmonious silence of heaven.' Both quotes via https://richardnilsen.com/tag/karl-albert-brull/

24 The most important work about the detailed circumstances of the genesis and premiere of 'Quatuor' is Rebecca Rischin, *For the End of Time* (Cornell University Press, 2006); regarding the audience of the premiere see pp. 61–70.

25 https: //www.irishtimes.com/culture/maybe-it-s-messiaen-s-moment-1.268117

26 I distinguish a 'reactionary' from a 'progressive' Nietzsche.

27 According to a late Cabalistic tradition, God gave up her/his omnipotence and omniscience, but he/she remained a voice in a heavenly council whose decisions determine the continuation of the world. God proclaims the consensus reached, being guided by the arguments and feelings of the council members who are witnesses, prophets, sages throughout the times. God can be overruled in council. I owe this cabalistic 'research poetry' to my old friend Norman Simms.

28 After Peter Hill and Nigel Simeone. *Messiaen* (Yale University Press, 2005), p. 172.

29 S. Jutta Georg, 'Ethics of the Body: Nietzsche and Lévinas' in *Perspektiven der Philosophie* 38 (1), 2012, pp. 343–61; and the Nietzsche chapters in Heinrich Schipperges' groundbreaking study *Kosmos Anthropos. Entwürfe zu einer Philosophie des Leibes* (Stuttgart, 1981).

30 *Truth is Symphonic: Aspects of Christian Pluralism*, tr. Graham Harrison (Ignatius Press, 1987). As the expanded title indicates, the treatise is primarily about Christian pluralism, but under the paradigm of symphonic music.

31 After Robert Sholl, 'The shock of the positive: Olivier Messiaen, St. Francis and redemption through modernity' in *Resonant Witness: Conversations between music and theology*, Jeremy S. Begbie, Steven R. Guthrie (eds) (Eerdmans, 2011), p. 163.

A Stand-up Mother

Ten years ago, I attempted to conquer the world. My nine-year-old son stayed behind with family, and I compressed my twenties into one August and went to the Edinburgh Fringe Festival with a solo show I'd rehearsed four times.

I was to be the star of my own sitcom—a sexy single twenty-something trying to navigate life (and love) in the big city. Mothers have plotlines, but target audiences, focus groups and demographics don't care about parenthood. Kids are boring, and so are the people who have them.

It's not a good sitcom if the sexy twenty-something can't have an affair to regret with Dave in HR because she can't go to after-work drinks because the after-school care programme charges fifty bucks if you're two minutes late. There's nothing to keep the viewer engaged if the sexy twenty-something is reading *Fox in Fucking Sox,* waiting for her child to fall asleep so she can eat ice cream in peace instead of taking E and pashing up bouncers.

The Hero's Journey—an oft-referenced, overused story archetype—is an individual pursuit that rarely involves children. Kids bog the hero down with childcare logistics.

I paid for my flights and accommodation in advance and had £300 to last the month. I was exhilarated by my recklessness. I was to be one of those poor students surviving on noodles—a charming, adorable, rite of passage—when it doesn't involve child neglect.

Until that August, I had never lived with adults my own age. I assumed it would be like season one of *Friends.* Clearly, I was Phoebe. My five Edinburgh flatmates were also performers, also unknown, also sexy twenty-somethings trying to navigate life (and love) in the big city.

*

My high school had one of those fancy mottos in Latin: 'Palma Non Sine Pulvere', which roughly translates to 'Please Don't Get Pregnant'. But I did, in my final year.

I had a baby before it was mainstream. Motherhood wasn't aspirational; it was failure. I opened letters from adventuring friends while trying to entertain myself. Once, I drew giant eyebrows on my son with Mum's eyeliner. Okay, more than once.

I did have options—the lady at the clinic asked, as if she had the power to grant wishes, 'What would you like to do with your life?'

'I'd like to write for television, please.'

'You can't do that with a kid,' she said, and pencilled me in for a termination. She made some phone calls and laughed nervously, 'They call me the abortion lady.'

All we had to do to 'get the ball rolling' was prove that having a baby would ruin my life, and it wasn't hard to do that. I'm grateful I had the option, but the thought of being naked waist-down in front of a doctor was terrifying.

I would like to point out that I had a baby because I didn't take my pants off.

This was clearly flawed reasoning, and you may wonder, did I go on to be the first person to give birth while wearing pants?

…?

…?

…?

No.

Pants came off, baby came out, and Mum drove us home in the old station wagon. I was overwhelmed and tired and scared—but actually happy to be a mum. This surprised me. I've always been more of a dog person.

My family gave me flowers. On the card, my sister drew a cartoon of a baby crawling through a pile of broken glass. Cartoon Sarah had no idea what she was doing; she'd dropped the baby and didn't even care. Cartoon Baby ate glass. I laughed, then burst into tears. Mum went back to New World to get a new card. My sister wasn't allowed to draw on that one.

After the first season with a newborn had passed, along came the season where I found myself getting defensive about my status as a young mother. I imagined myself as somehow different or better than other people in my situation. I reminded myself how surprised everyone was when I got pregnant. I was not that sort of girl. I was a good student, a good girl, a goodie good. Not like those other girls. I refused to join any support network targeted at teen mothers. I had nothing in common with these girls—apart from an illegitimate child and newfound role as a cautionary tale.

Instead, I went to a Plunket coffee morning for new mothers in the region. I couldn't drive, so Mum came along. I was closer in age to the newborn babies than half the women who were now my peers. I struggled to make conversation. I was embarrassed to exist. I ate fifteen Gingernuts and cried when I got back to the car. I never went back.

After that, I was in an episode entitled, 'The One with the Aggression'. Out in the wild, I anticipated the judgement of strangers. I stormed down the street with my boy in the pram, preparing angry monologues of exactly what I would say to strangers who I almost *hoped* would say something, just so I could unleash those negative voices swimming around my head:

'You think I'm a loser? You've never left Dannevirke. How about you remember this loser's face because one day I'll be famous. I'll be on *Shortland Street*, then *Coronation Street*, then there will be interviews with me in your *TV Guide* asking What's in my Beauty Bag, and I'll say my beauty secret is drinking lots of water, and there'll be my face as a photo clue in your stupid *That's Life* celebrity crossword puzzle because you're too thick to do the crossword in the newspaper.'

My comebacks were more aggressive than I was, and I never got to use one. It turns out that people are less judgemental in real life than they are in the comments section of *Stuff*. People who judged my situation did so in the kindest and most proper manner—behind my back.

To my face, everyone said I was doing an amazing job. The midwives, the doctors, my family, my friends' families—I got a round of applause every day that I didn't accidentally kill my baby. I'd inadvertently become the plucky underdog. It had its perks. Every minor achievement was met with surprise, congratulations. I was a success story for staying off P.

Then came the megalomania. The ambition. It wasn't good enough to lead a normal life. I had to beat the odds, race against the statistics, the reports that state:

> New Zealand has one of the highest rates of teenage pregnancy among OECD countries. This is of concern because teenage parents and their children are known to be at risk of medical, psychological, developmental and social problems. Medical complications for teenage mothers during pregnancy include anaemia,

hypertension, premature delivery and having low birth weight babies. Other known health risks for teenage mothers include drug and alcohol abuse, exposure to family violence and domestic abuse, sexual abuse, mental health problems and repeat teenage pregnancy. Children of teen parents have been shown to be at increased risk of developmental disabilities, behavioural problems and infant mortality. Long-term follow-up has also shown a higher risk of poor educational outcomes, depression, incarceration and continuation of an intergenerational cycle of teen parenting.

The day I turned twenty, I woke up, filled my adult lungs with air and skipped into the lounge: 'I'm no longer a teen mum!'

My sister looked up from her *Girlfriend* magazine, stared me dead in the eye and said, 'You'll always be a teen mum.'

Which is true. Because even now, twenty years later, the age at which I became a mother is still cause for alarm in those casual conversations which start with the weather and end with kids: 'You look too young to have a twenty-year-old?' They narrow their eyes, hold the silence and try to craft an elegant way to ask how old I was when I first gave birth.

'What are you in the Chinese zodiac?'

'Dog.'

'So, you were born in 1982, 83?'

Their eyes glaze over and I watch the cogs turning as they do the math. They need to know the exact birthing age so they can determine just how much scandal stands before them.

Was I legally allowed to have sex? Do I know who the father is? Am I still with him? How much of a role does he have? They imagine me, twenty years ago, eight months pregnant, untangling a phone cord and gossiping to Tiffany Jones instead of doing homework. They imagine the shame my parents felt— where did they go wrong? Rotten tomatoes thrown at the house, disappointed teachers, disgusted clergy, a quivering teen with a bulging belly who should've known better.

The interrogator is generally Caucasian, average height, middle-aged. The birthing age of others is very important to this demographic. My response was to cut the tension, to slip into a routine. A stand-up comic on a stage, nothing but a microphone and the ability to undermine herself to make other people feel comfortable.

'I'm from Dannevirke, if that explains it.' That always gets a laugh.

It's addictive, the response. The about-turn of a social situation where I masterfully place myself in control of the narrative. Pay me in laughter, applause. Pay me in love.

*

In the centre of Edinburgh, everything is made of castle. The roads are cobbled and rickety. Roller skates would break teeth. As you walk away from the centre, everything is made of *Coronation Street*.

I was a local. I ploughed through crowded streets, cursing at all the goddamn tourists stopping to listen to all the goddamn bagpipers or buy some goddamn tartan that represented the missing link between them and their Scottish ancestry.

My show was at 2.30pm. The people who came were killing time between lunch and the shows of people they actually wanted to see. At night, my venue was a nightclub.

When you buy a ticket to a show, you're engaged in a contract. The performer does their best to entertain you, and you do your best to be entertained. The act of buying a ticket is an act of trust. I was part of the Free Fringe, so neither tickets nor trust were exchanged. I had to win people over quickly, or they'd leave. The worst show of my life began like this. The room started full, but every thirty seconds, someone would stand up and walk out. It was contagious. I was in a psychological experiment.

As each person left, I became further and further detached from my body. My voice became shrill. I wanted the show to end. I started to cut out material on the fly, speed it up (the kiss of death) until I was a cartoon rat shrieking in the middle of an empty nightclub.

The few people who politely stayed till the end gave generous tips because they were concerned for my mental health. One was a reviewer.

I found out about my spectacular one-star review from my beautiful acquaintance, who spent that August performing to full crowds and rave reviews. I spent the rest of the trip pretending to be happy for her while she gleefully recounted to all who would listen how my show made the reviewer 'question the state of the comedy in New Zealand'. She returned from

Edinburgh with a talent agent. I returned with a maxed-out credit card, to a temp job at the Department of Labour. And my nine-year-old son.

*

These days I don't apologise or say crowd-pleasing one-liners. Now, when people say, 'You look too young to have a twenty-year-old!' I laugh and slap them playfully—a little too hard—on the arm, 'Aren't you a scream! I turn *fifty* next week.' I hold the silence. Then, if I'm ever concerned that I've exaggerated into fantastical realms, I attempt to pass the 'I'm in my fifties' test by complaining about my inconsiderate tenants who insist on using real picture hooks with *nails* in them, despite the fact it's clearly stated in the tenancy agreement they can only use 3M sticky hooks, even though they are ticking time-bombs where every picture on every wall is in danger of crashing to the ground in an undetermined timeframe—it could be a week, it could be a year—photos of their loved ones will crash to the floor and create a dent in the linoleum so I will then have to redo the *entire* kitchen floor because the current linoleum was discontinued in 1972 so it would be impossible to patch up a small bit. Obviously, it's coming out of the bond—but honestly, Susan, it's like they think it's their home or something.

I always felt that I became a mum the wrong way. That if I were older, I would be a better mother, I would have more financial stability, know what I'm doing, have an established career.

The girls who made fun of me at school now have kids. They're superheroes, warrior women and goddesses. They share photos of crinkled post-baby bellies that don't have stretch marks—they have 'tiger stripes'. They've calculated that motherhood pays four cents an hour. If you don't believe it, there are graphs. Data. Inspirational quotes. They are united by their belief that mothers are incredible. Motherhood is success.

We all did the same thing: had kids. But they did it the right way. So, they're allowed to complain. And they do. No one understands them. The blog posts are constant. The links, the memes, the videos, the photos, the identity. 'Why did no one warn us?'

We did. The warnings have existed as long as people could write. There are cave drawings of women with breasts like tentacles feeding litters of babies, throwing spears at each other's foreheads as an act of mercy.

I get no joy from their struggle—but my inner teenager enjoys watching them suffer.

I know it's not their fault. Sitcoms end when the cast settles down.

Ten seasons of a life worth watching, then the characters get married, have babies, move to the suburbs and are escorted off the network. Their apartment is disinfected to remove all traces of mediocrity so as not to infect the next generation of sexy singles navigating life (and love) in the big city. Maybe they are sent to that magical farm where dogs and horses go, shot in the head, boiled for glue. It really doesn't matter where they go or what they do, as long as they don't do it in public.

*

In Edinburgh, I didn't only find credit-card debt. I also found my husband.

My shows went well. I started to have fun. I made friends and went to karaoke. I came home at 3am to realise I'd forgotten my keys, so decided to see out the night in a bar for performers. There I met an Irishman who drunkenly called his sister that same night to tell her he'd just met his future wife and he was probably going to have to 'move to Australia or something.'

I left New Zealand to star in a sitcom, only to find I was in a romantic comedy. Maybe I wasn't a failure. Maybe I existed in a different format.

Thirteen years after my first son was born, I was pregnant again. This time around, I knew it was a good thing because in that split second after I took the test, there was nothing but excitement. I took a photo of the positive pregnancy test and sent it to my sister: 'I peed on this.'

It's very relaxing being pregnant when everyone knows how to react. I was openly congratulated for conceiving a child. It didn't make scientific sense. The exact same action had the opposite reaction.

But then came the bit where I started a competition between my current self and my teenage self. I had to prove that if Teen Mum Sarah could raise a kid by herself, then Thirties Sarah in a proper relationship would be one of those mums who gives birth, then runs a marathon while negotiating peace in the Middle East, writing the Great Novel and drinking smoothies laced with chunks of frozen placenta.

What do I know now?

Motherhood wasn't hard because I was young.

It was hard because it's hard.

All those grown-up mums in the coffee group were just as scared and clueless as I was. Except I looked great in shorts.

I feel bad that I was so hard on my younger self. I feel bad that I refused to connect with other young mothers. But how could I lean into an identity that is so openly scorned? People still think that a teenager can only get pregnant with semen samples from the entire first fifteen.

Having a baby young made me ambitious. I used to think this was an admirable quality, but now I'm less sure.

The Hero's Journey worships individualism, achievement, the plucky underdog, the person who doesn't quit, who beats Goliath, who doesn't say no, who keeps pursuing success without regard to balance, who never forgives and always wins in the end.

We are meant to aspire to this narrative. We are meant to keep up with these Joneses. We are meant to audition for these roles.

Now I wonder if motherhood and ambition are two parallel lines that should never meet. Ambition did not allow me to enjoy motherhood, even under ideal circumstances. Parenting was a career where I loved my colleagues but hated the job. It was one of drudgery, of insignificance. The ordinariness was repulsive.

These aren't aspirational feelings, but you can't be labelled a failure for becoming a mother and then expect to feel that motherhood is enough. You can't be fed a rhetoric that a baby is the worst thing that could ever happen to you—a demographic to be obliterated, a problem that requires task forces, legislation, intervention and declining trends—then believe you don't need to seek greatness in order to atone for living life in the wrong order.

Teen pregnancy—it's not for everyone. But perhaps the judgement of others is more damaging to a young person than a baby.

Without kids, I'd be crushed by bad reviews, resuscitated by praise. Always on the outside, looking in, nose pressed up against the window pane of other people's lives, fogging the window, my hand prints on glass.

So where can I put that drive, that desire to evolve? Do I cram it into a lunchbox next to Pinterest-worthy snacks? Do I force my children to learn tap dancing? Play rugby?

Instead, I make sub-standard school lunches, keep a tidy home (one day a week), work in government, catch public transport. I go to football and tolerate rock collections. I take my shoes off before jumping on the trampoline. I love my friends; one is my husband. I watch television, but don't need to be on it. My life won't win an Emmy, but it's a role worth playing.

REFERENCE

New Zealand has one of the highest … R. Johnson and S.J. Denny, *The Health and Wellbeing of Secondary School Students attending Teen Parent Units in New Zealand* (University of Auckland, 2007).

Mothers and Daughters

We all thought Mum would die first. Then Dad, with his new hips, would start to live his own life. Mum had a brain tumour—a meningioma. Her first operation went quite well, although the surgeon couldn't get all of the tumour out. But it was benign (such a misleading word), and he said she'd die of something else before it grew big enough to cause a problem—she was already seventy-eight. It grew back faster than the surgeon had predicted.

She rang me in Wellington. 'Your father's got a spot on his lung. They think it's pneumonia. Once he's over that, he'll have his hips done. So I'm going to have my operation soon, and then I'll be up and about by the time he needs me to look after him.'

A small knot formed in my stomach, but I pretended it wasn't there. She was deluding herself if she thought she'd be able to look after Dad after she'd had surgery. That tumour was mucking around with her thinking. At least Dad went to see the surgeon with her.

*

Mum was an only child, born in Blenheim during the early years of the Depression. She'd had two stillborn sisters, one older and one younger. Fay and Rosemary—I don't remember who was who. The younger sister was born and died in 1937 when Mum was six. When I asked Mum about her sisters in the last year of her life, she vehemently denied ever telling me that they had names. Why had she said they did, if they didn't? At the time, I thought it was the tumour scrambling her mind.

Mum said Nanna never saw her babies. She wanted Pop to see them, but he wouldn't. 'You'll always be at me to tell you what they looked like.' I tried to find their graves in Linwood Cemetery where I think they were buried but found only an unkempt section with little headstones marking little plots. None had names.

It's hard to get a sense of Mum's life with Nanna and Pop. Mum was born while they were probably still grieving for their first lost daughter. In photos from her childhood, she is alone or in the company of her parents and their friends. Occasionally she's with her cousins. 'My cousins, Diane and Marilyn, were the closest thing I had to sisters.' There are few photographs of Mum with her friends outside of school. 'I didn't really have close friends. I didn't know how to talk to people because Mum and Dad never talked to me. They got worried about me as I got older and they started taking in boarders, university students from out of town. That was how I got to know your father.'

Pop was an only child too. Mum didn't find out that her aunt Cissie was really her grandmother, Pop's mother, until the day of Cissie's funeral. It was 1947. Mum was sixteen. They were returning to the house in Cashel St, probably taking the side path to the back door, when a neighbour called out to Mum. 'I'm sorry to hear about your grandmother.' 'She wasn't my grandmother. She was my aunt.' 'No, dear. She was your grandmother.' Mum always acted out the neighbour's words, contorting her face into one of false concern. Years later, I searched the Birth, Deaths and Marriages records online. Cissie certainly was Pop's mother.

*

I flew to Christchurch to go with Dad and Mum to the hospital when she was admitted. She'd have the surgery later that day—there was no mucking around—and she'd possibly be discharged in a day or so. My niece, Bella, was one of the nurses on duty in the recovery ward. She promised to let us know as soon as Mum came out of surgery.

The surgery went well. Dad, my brother Din and I were allowed into the recovery ward, where Mum was starting to come round. We stood around her bed, relieved. But then, she started to shudder, then twitch and shake; she tossed around the bed like a woman possessed. The nurses were with her before we had a chance to call out. They shooed us out and set to work.

I don't know how long we waited or who came to tell us that they'd finally got Mum stabilised. Were we allowed back in then? I think so. We waited for the surgeon—a brusque woman, who pronounced her assessment of the situation, gave some orders and then disappeared, never to be seen or heard from again.

Mum wasn't good. She had a number of these seizures, which she was aware of while they were happening. She told us later she was terrified. I thought that the first one was going to kill her. After the surgery, her left side wouldn't do what she wanted and she couldn't walk. She was moved from the public hospital to Princess Margaret, a hospital that focused on rehabilitation. She hadn't needed this after the first surgery.

*

With Dad, we had fun. At the beach when we were small, he'd be in the water, carrying us and helping us jump the waves. Later, he taught us to body surf at Brighton and Taylors Mistake. Mum would sit on the beach, 'I don't want to get my hair wet or it'll go frizzy', and count her children over and over again. 'There's Annemarie, Gill, Mary, Mike, Din, Tim, 1, 2, 3, 4, 5 and 6.' Once when he'd traded in his car for a new Chrysler Valiant, Dad took me (and I think Mary and Mike) out for a test drive. On a back road near Oxford, his foot hit the floor. 'Let's see how fast it'll go, kids.' 'Faster, Dad, faster!' we shouted, standing up in the back seat.

As a small child, I followed Dad around the garden as he planted and tended the vegetables. There's a black and white photograph of him crouching over a line of seedlings with me on his back, legs dangling and arms around his neck. I remember that the home-knitted jersey I was wearing was a light green. Mum said, 'There never was a child as attached to her father as you.'

*

Dad died first. That spot on his lung wasn't pneumonia. I knew it even as the doctor talked about antibiotics, but I couldn't bear to raise it with Dad sitting beside me. I watched the hospital treat him for pneumonia (it didn't work), then they did a CT scan. We had to wait a week or so for the results and longer again to see his specialist. The scan showed what we feared. Then there was another week. Mum was in Princess Margaret, where the staff were trying to get her mobile and find the right balance of medication. We, Mum and Dad's children, took turns going with Dad to his appointments while the rest waited in the café at the boatsheds just across the river for the latest news. By the time Dad was diagnosed with stage four lung cancer, it was too late even for palliative treatment. I said, 'If you can't do anything, I'm taking him home.' The hospital sent a bed to Mum and Dad's house, brought around by a man called Colin, who had his own experience of losing someone to cancer. Nurses came twice a day to help look after Dad. They showed Mary and me how to top up the morphine pump. Mum came home to be with Dad. He died on a Friday, less than a week after I'd brought him home. Colin came back for the bed. 'That wasn't long,' he said.

Mum told me she didn't want anyone who was likely to cry to speak at Dad's funeral. 'I hate those funerals where lots of people get up and just weep.' She sewed her feelings up inside herself and turned inward.

*

I'm trying to remember what my mother was like when I was small. She'd had Annemarie eighteen months before I was born and Mary fifteen months after (then three little brothers arrived). Mum told me I didn't walk until I was eighteen months old. She was sick of trying to carry two babies around, so she eased me up with her foot. I've believed this for years, but recently I found my Plunket book. I walked at fourteen months. Why did she make up this story, and why did it get to me?

Mum had her hands full with six children born over ten years. She dedicated herself to looking after us. She cooked and baked—the tins were always full, but not for long. Once, frustrated at how quickly the baking disappeared, she hid a chocolate cake under her bed and then forgot about it. When she remembered, it had gone stale and had to be thrown out. She never did that again. She sewed and knitted for us and made wedding and bridesmaids' dresses. She'd put up the wooden playpen in the living room and set up her sewing machine inside: she couldn't have the grubby mitts of toddlers fingering that pure white material. She taught me and my sisters to sew. 'Did you measure that properly? The seam's not straight. Unpick it and do it again.' My sisters and I would buy fabric in town on a Friday night and compete for the sewing machine on Saturday so we could make something to wear that night. Eventually, she bought us a second-hand sewing machine, a shiny black Liberty, to share.

Nanna drove to our house almost every afternoon of my childhood, sometimes with Pop. She brought homemade cakes and biscuits to supplement

Mum's baking. I can't remember her helping Mum around the house, but she probably did. Nanna and Pop came to all our family picnics, and she'd be miffed if she heard that we'd been on an outing without her.

*

I'd given up my job as a lawyer in Wellington to look after Dad and then stayed for a few more weeks after his death to help Mum when she was discharged from Princess Margaret. It had been a simple decision; I couldn't have left my father. And I wasn't enjoying the job. Every time I had to tell someone something they weren't going to like, my heart rate would climb, and my breath would shorten. I'd rush to the loo and sit watching my breath move in and out while I tried to calm down.

Mum's condition improved for a while but then plateaued. She lost heart. She stopped doing her exercises. Her left hand started to shake. She needed a walking frame to get around and, later, a wheelchair when we went out. She sat on the couch with Molly, her British blue, on her knee and withdrew. At first, she ate chocolate and biscuits and ice cream and little else. I tried to get her to talk to me. She'd just look at me blankly. The house itself felt dead. Finally, I yelled, 'I loved him too. And I need you!' She roused herself for Molly and maybe for me.

If the carer was late, and they often were, I'd help her shower and dress. Sometimes I'd take her out in the car to Ballantynes or Merivale Mall, where she'd buy clothes she didn't need and often didn't wear. Sometimes she'd change her mind, and I or Annemarie would have to take whatever it was back to the shop. I hated the waste. I failed to see that she needed the distraction, the sense of being in charge of her own life that spending money gave her.

Living with her, I learned that she knelt by her bed every night to say her prayers and when she couldn't kneel, she'd say them in bed. Sometimes I read them to her. I learned that she always made her bed in the morning, placing her carefully folded pyjamas under the pillow. I learned that she was brave and determined. I hadn't spent so much time with my mother since I was a child.

I moved back to Wellington in need of a job but without the heart to sell myself to employers. I walked two or three hours every morning and spent the afternoons tidying up my CV and writing application letters for jobs I had no real interest in getting. I was going through my savings. After four months, I got a break, a job as a lecturer at Massey in Palmerston North. I spent two days a week, one semester a year, teaching environmental law to planning students. About once a month, I'd spend a few days in Christchurch. I'd stay with Mum. Take her out. Sort out any bills and paperwork. Run around doing her messages.

*

When I was twelve we moved to a two-storey weatherboard house in Bishop St and, about then, I started to pull away from my mother. I remember her reaching out to draw me onto her knee while watching an old Hollywood film on a wet Sunday afternoon. I slipped away from her. She must have been hurt. I'd started to be irritated by her; we'd niggle and snipe. We clashed more and more often—both hormonal in different ways, though I had no idea about her end of the process, and she would never have told me.

Once we were all at school, Mum got a part-time job behind the makeup counter at the PSIS shop, and later she worked at a bridal shop in New Regent St. 'Your father never asked how I spent the housekeeping and he never stinted, but I just wanted to have money I'd earned myself.' Looking back, I wonder if she couldn't stand the empty house.

At Canterbury University, I made new friends and had a boyfriend from outside the network of Catholic schools. 'I'm going to move in with Mark.' Silence. She turned to glare at me. 'Can't one of my daughters do the right thing?' She stormed out the kitchen door, slamming it after her. A ceramic pot I'd given her was hanging from the door handle. It fell. It shattered. It turned the tables. I remember yelling, 'You've broken it. You don't care!' But did that happen then or was that another earlier row? The anger fits. I also remember that it was me who charged out into the night. Or was that later, after I'd fought with Mark and we'd broken up? I remember walking up Bishop St to Bealey Ave, along Bealey Ave to Carlton Mill corner and Mark's new flat. Angry and upset, I couldn't go in and sat for a while by the river. I blamed her for that for years, even though he and I got back together and broke up again many times after that.

When I left for London in 1983, my friend cried in her mother's arms at the airport; I couldn't wait to get on that plane. Three years later, I got on a plane to come home. Scruffy and jaded, I walked out of the arrivals hall at Auckland Airport, and there was my mother; she'd flown to Auckland to meet me and bring me home. I was a bit put out, but thinking about it now makes me sad. All my life, I reacted to her attempts to hold me close by pushing her away.

*

Mum hadn't wanted to go into a rest home. She really wanted me to come and live with her, but I knew it'd destroy me—as a young adult I could manage only a few days staying with her before she got to me, and I'd be counting the days before I'd return to Wellington.

One Christmas, after a couple of weeks of respite care at Diana Isaac Retirement Village, she made the decision to move in. She settled in well to start with. She didn't have to worry about leaving the front door unlocked for carers or shuffling down the long hallway to answer the door. She got regular meals and could have a glass of wine. She didn't seem to mind that many other residents were no longer up to conversation. The honeymoon stage didn't last long. Soon she'd greet me with, 'Somebody get me out of this hellhole'.

The biggest wrench for her was giving up Molly. Her new owner let me pick her up occasionally and take her to see Mum for an afternoon. 'You'll tell me if anything happens to Molly, won't you?' When it happened, my sisters said, 'Don't tell her. She doesn't need to know.' 'But I promised.' And so I did. I rang from Wellington. 'Oh, oh. I can't talk about it,' and she hung up abruptly. All her buried grief spilled out in tears for Molly.

*

In their sixties, Mum and Dad travelled. Dad went to French classes, the gym, the office. Mum took up Italian. Years earlier, she'd joined the Mt Pleasant Pottery Club. She made quilts. She knitted for her grandchildren and helped my sisters out bringing up their three kids each, on their own. She and Dad bought a bach at Wainui, an hour's drive from Christchurch, so the family could enjoy holidays together.

Pop died, and a few years later, Nanna did too. After her funeral, we told stories and jokes about Nanna, teasing Mum until she burst into tears. 'She was my mother.'

Not long after the earthquakes, Mum told me she was jealous of us, her children, because we ganged up against her. 'You always stuck together. I had no one.'

*

That last year, she attended her oldest grandson's wedding and met her new granddaughter and first great-granddaughter. She celebrated her last St Patrick's Day, wearing the green on the day that a gunman murdered worshippers at two Christchurch mosques. She marked her eighty-eighth birthday at a family gathering. Her face was puffy and she seemed elsewhere.

There were no more outings. We'd sit and talk. She told me, 'I'm angry at Mum. She controlled my life. She never let me have friends of my own.' We talked about Nanna, the lost babies, postnatal depression. 'Yes. I remember her standing in the kitchen holding a large knife. She ran her finger along the blade and said, "I wonder what it feels like."'

I didn't ask her again about the babies' names. Instead, I found an article on the internet about stillborn children buried at Linwood Cemetery: 'It was believed that if the mother had any connection with the baby, it would make the grieving period longer and harder.' Then it talks of the burial: the child could be buried at the foot of an open grave or placed in someone else's coffin. The burial of Mum's younger sister is recorded at Linwood Cemetery, but I found no sign of her. Her grandmother, Cissie, is buried only a few plots from where she should be.

I suspect the babies didn't have names; Mum must have named them—a little girl desperate for sisters. Like Mum, I prefer to call them Fay and Rosemary.

There's so much more I would have liked to talk to Mum about. So much I'll never know now.

*

Mum was weepy, anxious, wanting to die, and then 'I'm jubilant!' when Annemarie walked in the door after a trip away. The palliative care nurse came and went. Mum's doctor adjusted her medication back and forth.

I'd visit, sit with her, work on my laptop as she dozed. I'd help her sip tea from a baby's cup until she couldn't keep it down, and later I'd moisten her lips with a little sponge. A few weeks before she died, she asked me, 'Do you think it's true?' 'Yes, of course, it's true.' I mentioned this to Father Simon who said her funeral mass at St Francis of Assisi. 'That happens a lot with people of strong faith. It's natural. They're frightened.'

Of course, she was frightened. No wonder she couldn't see that I was tired, that Annemarie was run ragged. She was a woman facing the end of her life and she couldn't look away.

*

The last time we spoke I'd gone in to say goodbye as I had one final class to teach in Palmerston North. She said, 'But I'm dying.' 'I know Mum. I'll be straight back.' What possessed me to leave? When I returned a few days later, she was mostly unconscious, though she stirred once and said my name. I sat with her. I met Mark for coffee and then sat with her some more. As I was leaving that evening, I met Tim and his older son coming in. 'Stay a bit longer. We'll drink some wine and keep her company.'

I left my sister's house early the next morning and drove through rush-hour traffic and roadworks to see Mum. My phone rang as I stood at the nurse's station. It was Annemarie, 'The nurse has just rung. Mum has died'. I went into her room. She was still warm; I felt her body cool as I held her hand. Soon my brothers and sisters started to arrive.

The funeral director asked what to put down on the death certificate for Mum's occupation. Tim said, 'Artist'. She'd have been pleased with that. We took her to Wainui to bury her with Dad, looking out over Akaroa Harbour towards the heads. Sons and daughters, grandsons and granddaughters, we all took turns on the end of a shovel and buried her ourselves.

*

I have a photograph that Pop would've taken in the 1960s. Mum and Dad stand at the back against the pink summerhill stone wall of our house. Dad is holding Din. Tim, the baby, would've been inside asleep in his cot. Annemarie, Mike, Mary and I are standing in front of our parents. We three little girls are all wearing the same dress but in different colours. Mum made them. I'm leaning into my mother. She has her arm around me.

This essay was partly inspired by Helen Garner's 'Dreams of Her Real Self'.

REFERENCE
It was believed that … Kete Christchurch 'Still-born children in Linwood cemetery', Friends of Linwood Cemetery Charitable Trust: http://ketechristchurch.peoplesnetworknz.info/site/topics/show/2070-still-born-children-in-linwood-cemetery

CLAIRE MABEY

Holy Smokes

Cigarettes offer (or used to offer) the writer a great range of metaphoric possibilities. They have lives and deaths. They glow and they turn to ashes. They need attention. They create smoke. They make a mess.

I have always been fascinated by cigarettes. Everyone in my family smoked. At funerals and Christmases in Pahiatua I'd eye up the packets of Holiday menthols and Marlboro Lights and Pall Malls. I knew where each packet was located on each body. In the back pocket of my grandad's faded green pants. In the bruised handbag of my aunty Eenie. Lying near the ashtray on the kitchen table. And we all knew about the packets hidden in the cupboard underneath the phone and the notepads and the maps. My cousin once took me out the back of Grandad's house where the grass tickled our knees and there was a stream with real frogs living in it. She pulled a single cigarette and lighter from her jeans pocket and sat in the grass like a wolf. The smoke streamed out her nostrils and I was mute with jealousy. Dragon woman. Wolf lady.

I declined her offer to try a puff for the first time.

'Good,' she said, 'they'd all kill me if they found out.'

I think they'd have thought it was funny. That the older cousin was corrupting the younger one just like the older people corrupted the young people all the way through. Family fires get started, nurtured, and left to smoulder through the generations to skew vision and fuel strange stories. Sometimes I picture myself when I'm old, transformed into Gertrude Stein, puffing away on black cigars. Mischievously rewriting all the histories, stamping out all the old fires and arranging the kindling for new ones. There's something permissive about old age. And something permissive about art.

While I was in my early twenties and studying at Vic I worked at City Gallery. I was a 'visitor host' and had the Sunday morning shift. More than once

I was still drunk when I arrived for work. So I'd wallow in the slow pace of my one job, which was not to let anyone fuck with the art. I'd take a novel with me and read while I was meant to be standing alert. Once, upstairs, I stood in a room full of Guy Ngan absorbed in *The Catalogue of the Universe* by Margaret Mahy. A few pages in, I became aware of a sturdy woman standing and staring at me. I smiled at her, attempting a welcoming 'hope you're enjoying your gallery experience' kind of look. She didn't smile back. The next day all of us visitor hosts got a memo from our boss, Kate, asking us not to read while on duty. I later discovered that the woman was the director of the gallery, Paula Savage. Hers is a name I think about in the same way I ponder the endless indecision of 'Mabey'.

I got to know each exhibition intimately. Guy Ngan, Sriwhana Spong, Patricia Piccinini, Michael Smither, Elizabeth Thomson, Lonnie Hutchinson, Tony Lane. I paced around them on my party-worn boots raking over every speck, every letter in the captions, trying to find something new each time.

After all the years, it's the *Michael Smither: The Wonder Years* exhibition that shuffles closest to the front of my mind. The stolid yet luminous qualities of the people, the rocks, the water and the buildings. The frightening truth of the children, their poses and their games. The spasming, wounded flesh of St Francis in the ghostly grass. The unmoving stare of a nude Elizabeth Smither.

But it's not the painting so much as a line of text that has fused to the language still turning over in my head. Somewhere, printed on one of the walls of that exhibition was the line: 'the holding and carrying of fire'. The phrase sat within a paragraph about cigarettes, though I can't remember a painting in which anyone was smoking. That line articulated precisely what I have always been drawn to and can never let go of: cigarettes enable humans to make, hold and carry fire. The cave lady in me has her eyes fixed and her fingers twitching for that smoking stick.

Trouble is I've never been a successful smoker. My first real stint was a ritual study break on the verandah of my third student flat in Dunedin. My flatmate Fiona (seasoned and addicted) and I would pull polar fleeces on and creep out onto the worn weatherboards and sink into the rotten old couch that lived there. Fiona would hand me the weightless, smooth column to place between my lips. Then she'd pull out the lighter that lay like a tiny eel in the cave of the cigarette packet. Her movements were so enviably practised, so fluid. The lighter would make a small rasp and we'd puff and suck until we had the glow.

It was a quiet ten minutes. Squinting out across the city, I'd watch the snaking column of low cloud that often nosed its way into the harbour. I enjoyed the distance from the essays I had to bang out every week. It was peaceful. It felt adult. The methodical ritual warding off the world-weariness that we had yet to experience. I wanted to relish the harsh taste wafting down my throat. I wanted to be cool about it.

But I couldn't stick at it. Not like Fi could. The tar seemed to settle in my lungs too easily. Like the cancer was rubbing its hands together with glee, gloating 'I've got a soft one here, boys!' After a while, I'd just take my cup of tea out there and be content with second-hand drifts.

I tried smoking again when I lived overseas. One summer me, Fi, and two other friends travelled around Italy. We developed a taste for Campari and Fi would buy packets of Vogues. Long, thin cigarettes clearly targeted at those who prefer their smoking to be vaguely glamorous. The four of us would sit, puffing and sipping, and sweating in the high summer heat. We smoked in queues while we waited to see famous artworks. I'd finally arrive and swing between disappointment and awe. I loathed the hypocrisy of the Vatican but when I stood in front of Michelangelo's *Pietà*, Mary overwhelmed me with her immense, capable embrace of a parent's worst nightmare.

On the Cinque Terre we got told off for dropping cigarette butts out the window of our rented apartment. They were discovered nestled in the grass by the man who owned the place. I was ashamed of our carelessness. Our stay there had been the most nourishing of the whole journey: inside, the apartment was cool and outside there was a path that led down to the miraculous Ligurian Sea. I'd given up smoking again by then and instead ran the pathways between the rubbly, colourful villages while everyone else slept in.

I never managed to make smoke rings. Or breathe like a dragon as my cousin did in the long grass near the stream with the real frogs.

Yet, these days, I smoke daily in my head. I crave. The tips of my fingers twitch for ghost smokes. I have a potent memory of sitting in the corner of a dark pub with a whisky and my grandfather's silver cigarette case stuffed with rollies. Chaining them. Writing. Surrounded in fragrant clouds like I'm Janet

Malcolm in her unable-to-write-without-cigarettes phase. Nodding to people I recognise: musicians, artists, extremely attractive philosophy students. But there's me hovering around watching her. She's someone else.

She's a composite of the images of smoking I've compiled over many years from books, from art, from movies, from my family, from my friends. In *The Catalogue of the Universe* by Margaret Mahy there's a chapter called 'Mrs Potter rolls a cigarette'. In this chapter the son, Tycho, analyses his mother, Mrs Potter's, smoking while they talk about the complexities of love, sex and happiness (they have a close relationship). He observes:

> *Just for a moment, a different personality seemed as if it might be about to break through, something less cozy, even slightly raffish, much more the personality of a woman who liked to roll her own cigarettes. Perhaps it was to placate this tougher self that she smoked at all.*

And moments later:

> *Tycho watched her management of her cigarette with pleasure, enjoying the contrast between her cool, quick folding of the fragile fluttering paper around the tobacco (something she could do with one hand like a shearer or road man) and the flowery summer suit and apricot frill to her blouse.*

Why is it that smoking transforms a person? Allows us this kind of slant view like an Instagram filter. Sometimes it feels to me that watching someone smoke is perving on something that should remain private. People change in those few minutes preceding the act, during the act, the moments afterward. The mouth is preoccupied with the ritual lift and pull. The brain is washed with chemicals. The person crosses out of time and into something else: a greyer dimension. Margaret Mahy suspends us over this phenomenon: the private observations of the private ritual; the pervasive, compulsive act of making and controlling small fires. She conjures, perfectly, how a son's view of his mother wobbles as though he's seeing her through a heat wave: the honed craft of her smoking is like a portal into another Mrs Potter, adjacent, but not separate to the mother/wife dimension. I wonder if Jesus watched Mary smoke and realised who she really was. More than the mother of god.

I was reading the novel during the year I worked at City Gallery for a paper on Margaret Mahy and Maurice Gee's fiction for young readers, with Professor

Kathryn Walls. It must have been this chapter that prompted Kathryn to say that 'someone should write a thesis on smoking in New Zealand literature.' At that time I was also in the art history department trying to figure out what to write a dissertation on. I was tossing up between something on Rita Angus and the self-portrait or the fourteenth-century abbess Hildegard von Bingen and the relationship between her writing and her visual art. I went with Hildegard but Rita's staunch gaze is always, regretfully, in my periphery. A vision in a camel coat and emerald scarf, Rita scolds me for not chasing the fragrant trail of smoke she wields so effortlessly.

Am I writing this for unfinished business then? For Rita. For Kathryn. For Mrs Potter and Tycho?

This is the culmination of Tycho's observations in the cigarette chapter in *The Catalogue of the Universe*:

> *The cigarette hung a little on her lower lip. Tycho and Richard always enjoyed seeing it do that. It was a thin, uneven cigarette and, quite innocently, she looked like an uncertain beginner smoking a joint and doing it wrongly.*

Accidental wrongness. It's a state I consider often when I consider myself as Mum. I remember the agonising shame I'd feel at my parents' myriad wrongnesses. I imagine, with bitter-sweet amusement, what pains I will cause in years to come. I wonder if I will ever notice that my child's clothes smell of tobacco. If the urge to make and carry fire will prove too strong for him to resist. I wonder if I will watch him and see another self. I wonder if I would ever join him.

When a friend, a dad, lights up outside a writers' festival party it catches me out. There, suddenly, is that prismatic view: another version of him I rarely see. I drag the second-hand smoke into my nostrils. My cousin in reverse. For a second, all the smoking Claires in my head debate whether I should ask him for one. But I haven't smoked in a decade. The moment I do the burn of it hurts. It obliterates the fantasy. The pang in my lungs says, 'You're not Gertrude Stein'.

All I really want is to hold on to the tiny fire. To slow down and spend a cigarette-sized portion of time in the in-between. To shift my perspective.

I'm writing this smouldering with burnout. I've always needed art. But my way with it is getting strained with overuse. Too much time spent in the back end of the administration of it: trying to create spaces for people to gather around art like hands around a barrel of fire. The tedium of talking to people in office towers who tell me they understand the state of it because they're in a band that plays once a year at the Tinakori Fair. Too many spreadsheets. It has turned me anxious, nostalgic, craving cigarettes.

I am craving time. As though each length of cigarette is ten minutes gazing out from the porch. Ten minutes with my cousin. Ten minutes with my friends in Italy in our twenties. Ten minutes' pause on being a parent. Art has a similar effect. Music, reading, gallery pacing: they allow the expansion and tanglement of time. My brain turns supple. Moveable. I consider the concept of tūrangawaewae and know that it's not something that I have or understand. I often feel like I'm not really here. I'm still wandering around assessing all of the possibilities. Like I haven't been born. Like god has tipped me out into the options tank and has left me there, bumping into things and only occasionally glimpsing myself in the glass.

Is that the work of art? To help us slide around the land of potential?

It's Bob Dylan's eightieth birthday. I've binged his albums all day, travelling back and forward and sideways. I loved him as the sponge-like, earnest, soft-cheeked troubadour. I loved him more as the mildly unhinged performance artist on the road. He's old and the man has still very much got it.

I worry that we Dylan fans are all the same. A bit sad. Sliding vinyl out of sleeves looking for the something he has that we just don't. Bob slips through the nets while we circle the tank.

He's also one of the most captured smokers on the planet. A Google image search throws up tiles of black and white: his shaggy cigarettes held languidly in his long-nailed fingers. His hair must have reeked, his clothes must be so comforting. I'd like to step into them like I used to step into my grandparents' house and be immediately surrounded by lamb roast and tobacco. I wonder if smoking helped Bob write. Piles of ash marking piles of type-written lyrics.

I recently took a creative writing class at the IIML. A group of fourteen of us wrote short stories with the teacher William Brandt. The class was a collection of vibrant, shy, young, wise, mothers and children. Almost every one of us, at some point, wrote a character who smoked.

Smoking inside was made illegal in 2004 in New Zealand and most of my classmates would have been little children, the youngest just toddlers, at the time. I moved to Europe in 2009 and walked back into centuries of smoking inside. My landlady in Belgium (whom I fictionalised in a story for the class) used to burst into our house and talk to me in Flemish with her cigarette waggling between her lips. I didn't have much chance of understanding her at the best of times. But the language of the cigarette was exactly the same. The goldfish in my favourite Belgian pub swam through dull grey water and I remember stroking the lumps of cancer that speckled the pub cat's gingery ears.

In 2014, while I was still in smoke-filled Europe, my partner's brother, an oncologist, emailed me: 'Please tell me it's a pen and not an elegant cigarette', he wrote.

He was referring to a show I was advertising called Women of Letters. It was an event created by Australian writer/producers. A line-up of women were invited to write a letter on a theme and then read it aloud to the live audience. The Women of Letters logo was a silhouette of a woman holding a smoking pen to her lips. One of the founders has it tattooed on her arm. To me it's perfect. The holding and carrying of fire. The power of the pen.

Tobacco control occupied much of my brother-in-law's time. I understood his concern but resisted it. There *is* danger in writing. Even more when you have to read a letter, the most intimate of literary artefacts, out loud to strangers. There's enormous power too: the crowd was with the women all the way, laughing, crying, leaving the venue with hearts swelling and ghosts of their own unleashed. But there can be a profound personal risk.

We did four years of Women of Letters before the whole thing folded. Something irreparable happened between the two creators and the event evaporated between them.

Perhaps I am writing this for the things that don't survive?

My cousin died in a car accident when she was sixteen years old. It wasn't very long after she had showed me her smoking skills. I remember sitting near my aunty, her mother, at the wake. One of my uncles sat across from us with his packet of cigarettes on the table. He was ashen. He told me I shouldn't ever smoke, that it was a dickhead's game. My aunty said she felt like she was in a dream.

I worry that my memories are turning to dreams. They take flight and hover in an expanse of time as deep as the night, and grow feathers. My memories aren't as reliable as the stars. They're as fluid as smoke. The thing that holds still, just, is the art. Rita's portrait, Hildegard's visions, Bob's songs, Margaret's books. They destroy linear time. I hook myself up to music, books and paintings and try to find something solid among them to stand upon.

In the gallery, my hours as visitor host could crawl by. The lack of sleep would start to work its devilish tricks. I'd fret about the things I must have said or done that I couldn't quite recall. I'd start to panic about the reading I hadn't finished. The essays I hadn't started. I'd grow increasingly sure that my skin smelled of the night before—the sweet, toxic mess of cheap drinks.

But the opportunity to simply stand and watch allowed me to log careful, slow minutes that somehow circle back on me. Watchful, interrogating, meditative. I saw the way all of the artists' lives were arranged across the white walls in the temperature-controlled rooms. The way the visitors were reverent. Like we were all congregating in a church to access our ghosts by contemplating images that might speak of them. Life hung still. Cared for. Everything was in place to ensure survival, continuation, renewal. Hope, even.

It's no surprise that smoking has made a comeback during the pandemic. Existential threat breeds anxiety. A fair bit of turning inwards. But I think it's more: the temptation to hold and carry fire, to trick ourselves into stealing time, stepping out of time, is too much. There's wrongness in it: poison, deceit. We're creatures both drawn to and repelled by fire. A deep conundrum. And yet little white sticks appear where all my favourite art is, where all my favourite people are.

Janet Malcolm has just died of lung cancer. I know her writing will enjoy a resurgence now she's gone. On the one hand, time is kept still, extended, by a person putting their art into the world. To weave among us. Work its way in and expand. And on the other, there is never enough time with the things and the people we love. Or not enough of the right kind of time with the things and the people that captivate the parts of us that move differently to the minute-by-minute.

In the end, all I know is that If I could paint myself into permanence in an emerald scarf with a cigarette between my fingers, I would. And If I could refract the world like Gertrude Stein did while smoking black cigars, I would. And If I could roll a cigarette with one hand like Mrs Potter, I would. And If I could travel back in time and have my first smoke with my cousin, let her teach me to blow smoke through my nose to the soundtrack of tiny, impossible frogs, of course, I would.

This essay was previously published in November 2021 as 'I'm craving a smoke. I'm craving time' in The Spinoff: *https://thespinoff.co.nz/books/28-11-2021/claire-mabey-on-the-magical-pull-of-cigarettes*

REFERENCES

Cigarettes offer … Janet Malcolm, *Forty-One False Starts: Essays on artists and writers* (Farrar, Straus & Giroux, 2013).
Just for a moment … Margaret Mahy, *The Catalogue of the Universe* (J.M. Dent, 1985).
Tycho watched her management … Ibid.
The cigarette hung a little … Ibid.

CLAIRE MABEY

This Dark Country
Being an account of an 'anonymous character which is baffling and puzzling in the extreme'

FEVER

I no longer understand my own brain. It is being held underwater.

Everything floats. My cough sounds bigger on the inside. Like the phlegm is losing its mind inside a stony jail, rattling off madness all day and most of the night. Only when the brightest stars outlast the pinkening sky will it desist. There will be a moment of rest. Inside and out. A stillness beyond stillness as the trees and grass, the winds, rally for another day. Then the sun will journey at pace and the spiked energy will twitch and build into a fevered dance all over again.

FEVER

My son has thrown such a tantrum that his skin has taken on the look of a Lucian Freud painting: blotched, reddish pink in patches and greencream in others.

'I will smash the boat! Pull out all the plugs! There will be no swimming!'

I am in awe of his propensity for damage. At three years old his capacity for upset is bigger than he is. It takes over our house, electric, roiling and thrashing.

MUSIC

It is sleeting outside. In Island Bay. I pick up my purple ukulele and look up my saved songs on the Guitar Tabs app. I select the one that makes me cry the easiest: 'Wide Lovely Eyes' by Nick Cave.

MUSIC

My ukulele is out of tune. My three-year-old grabs at the little black knobs just before I reach out to play, every time.

I tune it with the easy online uke tuner and am grateful that it *is* easy. The two notes wobble against each other until I am successful in nudging the vibrations in line. I wonder if Nick Cave ever plays the ukulele. I wonder if Nick Cave has ever had to use the easy online uke tuner. I wonder if I look a bit like Nick Cave when he twists at the knobs on his guitar.

'Wide Lovely Eyes' is easier to play than I expect it to be. But I don't cry. Instead, I realise I should be singing 'Glass, Concrete and Stone' by David Byrne because I sound better when I sing it and the lyrics are optimistic. They're about going somewhere.

I get up and look out the window at the sleet. I feel nothing. Not even surprise. I consider opening the door to stand in it. The cold might help. At the very least it'll cause my eyes to water and so offer me the sensation of crying.

MUTANT RAT STORY

I notice a large clump of something lying across the gutter on the road below. A gutter monster. I'll point it out to my son when he calms down and I will make up a story about a mutant rat that only emerges when it snows once every ten years. My son will tell me it's just sticks but I'll insist that I saw it move. He will look again and then he will be a flurry of ecstatic pointing and yelling because he will see it move too.

SPYING

I have a clear view into one of the bedroom windows of the green weatherboard house below us. I like this house because they seem to have a productive vegetable garden and they used to have chickens. I observe the growth of the cabbages planted in rows. The raspberry frames are a pleasing blend of pragmatic and stylish.

WORSE SPYING

When I'm in our kitchen at night I glance over the houses of our neighbours. I enjoy the way the lights slowly turn on as the sky darkens. Like a series of signals flowing from one cluster of people to the next. Sometimes I feel guilty about my vantage point. But when I analyse the driver in my mind, I am confident that most of the time there is nothing morally dubious in my intentions. The greenhouse is simply the most interesting. There's often a teenage girl sitting on her bed, her laptop on her knees, just like me.

REALLY BAD SPYING

Once I watched her take a selfie. It was a very quick, natural movement. Like an animal twitching its ears. Every time I see someone taking a selfie, I think about Nick Cave. Or really his son, ---- Cave, who died from his injuries after falling while taking a selfie. I think about Susie Cave and what she makes for dinner and if she cries in the shower or when she is dreaming up ideas for clothes. Susie Cave designs the most beautiful dresses for her fashion label, The Vampire's Wife. Not that I've ever tried one on. I just look at them on Instagram and think about what happened until my eyes water. And I wonder if Nick cries in his studio when he's making music and writing responses to letters. He is a terrific letter writer. Not so remarkable, given his other writing.

SNAP OUT OF IT

What if Nick and Susie Cave sense me searching inside their heads like a creeping headache? I am so superstitious that I can't concentrate for worry that I am invoking something beyond my control. That I'm inviting a dialogue that I have no business to participate in. I can't write the child's name. I don't want to make that gesture, out of fear and respect. To bring him here is too bold. I want to be light as a butterfly with my love and my concern. These black marks on the digital page are the invisible lift and flap of my wings. Imperceptible waves. Silent waving. Why am I like this? Do I think that my heartache is the clumsy tread that will snap the stick and alert the monster that I am following him around this dark country? That I will reveal myself, defenceless, to the figure with the scythe, shadowy as a funnel of smoke, who will shunt its empty, hungry eyes toward me and my family?

I should go for a run and try not to think about death. Particularly the death of a son.

NO REALLY, SNAP OUT OF IT

But it is so cold and my chest and ears still sound waterlogged from the virus that won't leave me or my family alone. And yet running is the only thing that

I think of that could snap me out of this. I'd be reluctant at first, pulling on my tights and socks, unfurling the tight running bra over my breasts. But once out the door I would be ok, my legs would know what to do. I might hesitate over which route to take, whether to go by bush or by road, but I wouldn't stop running until I was home again.

ROBIN HYDE

The waves are supposed to be outrageous today. I could jog down the track that links our road to the park in Houghton Bay and stand too near the shoreline and risk being swept away. I imagine Robin Hyde being swept away in Island Bay. The idea is in black and white. I am not sure if the face that I see really is Robin Hyde's face.

THE SON

Ovingdean Gap is a 500-foot cliff in Brighton. One of those cliffs with chalky white soaring heights and green grass waving at the top. You see them on British crime dramas or in *Far from the Madding Crowd* when the sheep leap to their deaths.

That's how Nick Cave's son, ----, 'a bright, shiny, funny, complex boy' died. He fell over Ovingdean Gap.

MY SON

When I close my eyes at night, I see my son in various, precarious positions. Leaning out of windows, perched on the top of a high fence looking down at the concrete, tumbling down the stairs in our own steep back yard, falling from the gods in the Opera House after a boisterous tussle with a friend. I sit bolt upright in bed and gasp and grip my t-shirt. The one I can't sleep in because I'm imagining the death of my only child. This is the strongest feeling I have. Terror.

THE SON

---- Cave was a twin. I imagine the surviving twin at home now, listening to music with the shadow of his brother by his side. The smell of him. Perhaps he is wearing some of ----'s clothes. They are presumably of similar build.

MY SON

I wanted to have twins. To offer them to each other. Instead my son is offered the clothes of twins. My friend had two sons born together and now my son is the beneficiary of their hand-me-downs. Two of everything. One for the ruin, one to keep a little nice so it can be passed on again. I thought perhaps my lifelong dream of becoming Anne of Green Gables was likely to come to fruition through the conception of twins. Anne was destined for them. I feel further away from Anne than ever. I will only have one child to her six. Although her first baby, Joyce, died after only a few hours. Anne must always have felt that she had one less child than she should have.

BAD MOTHER MERMAID STORY

I need to go running and try to think about something else. Island Bay is called that because there is an island, Tapu Te Ranga, perched in the water directly across from the beach. The waves hit the island's back and massage its sides. Once Upon A Time, I tell my son, a family stole a boat and rowed to Tapu Te Ranga, to have a picnic. They took cake, and some lemons and sparkling water, and sandwiches and apples.

'Not floury ones!'

'No, not floury ones.'

Their picnic blanket was old and sturdy and had crumbs on it from all the other picnics people had eaten on it over the years.

They rowed to the island and set up their picnic by the rockpools. After a little while of quiet eating they heard a beautiful sound. It was a voice singing in a language they hadn't heard before. The mother looked over the shoulder of the little boy and saw a mermaid sitting on a rock. She had bright red hair and a tail as green as kākāpō feathers. Slowly, so as not to frighten her, the mother stood up and asked the mermaid if she'd like a piece of cake. The mermaid said, 'yes please' and flipped herself over to them.

'But how would she walk?'

My son is a pragmatist. And I'm too tired to elaborate. Too bored of my own dull mind to finish the story. The mermaid is ill-formed, the flipping is awkward, she'd have to half drag herself over the sharp rocks with her hands and then that would probably hurt her tail, probably graze her scales off in places. The weather is closing in on the mother and child and I think they should blink and be transported home again without the bother of rowing the little stolen boat. I play 'Tangled Up in Blue' on the ukulele and wonder if the red hair in the song is natural or dyed.

NICK CAVE MERMAID STORY

In Nick Cave's 'Wide Lovely Eyes', he sings of mermaids hanging from street lights by their hair.

I wander quietly down this ruined street looking at the dead mermaids. I wonder what kind of mind hangs mermaids by their hair. But I can see them and it makes sense. So I must have that kind of mind, too. The streets are dark but the moon is full and its light makes a glimmer of the mermaids' luminous scales. Their hair, being very long, is tangled and their necks are stretching and broken with the weight of their half-human bodies.

'Wide Lovely Eyes' is an exceptionally good tune. To me, one of the most beautiful of Nick Cave's songs. The melody rises and falls like gentle, swollen waves. And it runs to a satisfying end, rolling strongly over and into you before ebbing away.

I see the woman with her bare feet, the waves softly touching her toes, her shoes tidy beside her, no longer useful. Her lover is watching from the window. His long fingers blur with his waving. His heart is shattered. The mermaids are no longer welcome. She must leave to avoid the fate of the others. But in her wake is the idea of happiness. A dinner party of smiles and light stories about the funny things that happen to us at work, on family holidays, how our ageing parents can never get the hang of all their technologies.

BAD GIRL ANNE

I reread *Anne of Green Gables*. What strikes me now is how emotional she is. Anger is accessible, ecstasy is accessible, irritation is accessible. The author gives Anne full permission to wake up in any mood. Anne is allowed to have a thoroughly shitty day where everything goes wrong. She is often vexed, sometimes wise, always loved.

Anne fades into the background of her story as she gets older and has children. By the sixth book the story is barely hers. Instead, we follow the trials and tribulations of her twins, her eldest, her youngest, the middle child. We follow the boys into the First World War and feel the pain of death once again when Walter, the poetic gentle one, is killed.

Anne was always so good at dreaming. I wish L.M. Montgomery had written Anne's crone years. What her inner world might still have been capable of. I could use a mentor. I could use a tired mother's mind to inhabit.

TWITTER
I pick up my phone and send out a tweet: 'Favourite @NickCave songs?'

MERMAID TWITTER
I haven't left the house in some days. *Why would you?* The mermaid says silently. She floats around my brain flipping her tail and turning in loops like a seal. *Look at where you live,* she gestures. The grey, the swirl, the relentless energy. It's all trouble and worry and raincoats.

STORM
I should be out in it. Gather some energy. Make a memory. Nick Cave would enter the storm. He would seek the experience. I did once go on a long walk in a thunder-and-lightning storm. My friend Zoe and I were living in Greece, in a monastery. We helped the sisters with their large and verdant gardens. The weather didn't look good but we set off anyway. We wanted to find the little cave where the monastery's founding father first came to settle the community. We did find it. There wasn't much to see, more to marvel at how someone could have carved out a life in such a dark, remote little hole. Really only people with faith could pull it off, I thought. We got lost on the way back and found ourselves high on the mountain, in a clearing so close to the sky I thought perhaps we'd crossed into a portal. The lightning was so close and the thunder so loud we felt it rummaging through our bodies. The rain was enormous and warm. We screamed and laughed halfway between excitement and panic. It was dangerous, what we did. The nuns were waiting for us wringing their kind hands. I felt bad for a little while but in the end I am glad we have the memory of the eye of the storm.

TWITTER

These days I seek Twitter to comfort me and so I sink lower into the water.

Lots of people reply that they like 'Higgs Boson Blues'.

I do not even care. I should delete Twitter. Fuck Elon Musk. Fuck them all.

FEVER

I've had another chest infection. For three nights I shivered and hugged my grandmother's blanket close to my chin. I tracked the sensation of the virus' descent from my throat to my lungs. Such a familiar possession. Since having a child I've been sick so often it's the state more familiar to me than being well. Being unwell saps my energy, drains the colour from my face and the too-familiar worlds I inhabit now. Home, work, Cuba Street.

BAD MOTHER UKULELE MUSIC

I play 'Wide Lovely Eyes' on the ukulele and manage to make it sound dull and lifeless. It's not your fault, I tell the ukulele. It's not your fault, I tell Nick Cave.

ROBIN HYDE

I pick up my copy of *The Godwits Fly*. I got it at Persephone Books the last time I was in London. Robin Hyde suffered a lot of pain. Injuries, mental illness, the loss of children.

Robin Hyde lost two sons. Her first to death just days after birth. His name was Robin Hyde and that was the name she continued to use for her literary work. She lost her second son to the patriarchy. She had to adopt him out. The father of the tiny boy was married and told her she should pay for half the abortion.

JOAN DIDION AND DEATH

Late at night, after my son is finally asleep, I watch the Joan Didion documentary on Netflix. Her skin is so translucent you can see her veins. Grossly thick. She says something about writing what you're afraid of. That if you write what you most fear then maybe the hope is that it won't happen to you.

NICK CAVE AND DEATH

Nick Cave wrote 'Wide Lovely Eyes' a long time before the death of his child. But I wonder if he wrote it as some kind of talisman. A warning to the world that the end of beautiful, complex things should not come to be. Or at least, when they do, there will be a way to imagine they have simply fled back to where they are able to exist as themselves away from this hard world.

NICK CAVE AND SUSIE CAVE AND DEATH

Since the death of ---- Cave both Nick and Susie Cave have created exquisite things. I think of them often. Shovelling beauty at the black hole of sudden death.

VIRGINIA WOOLF AND DEATH

On 3 April 1941, the writer Sylvia Townsend Warner wrote in her diary:

> *A very noisy evening. We have lost Benghazi to the German advance. Today the news that Virginia Woolf, missing since Friday, is now presumed drowned in the Sussex Ouse.*

Virginia Woolf's death always comes as a shock. First the vanishing. Then the stones in her hands before they are dropped into her pockets. The way they bump against her thighs as she strides into the rushing water. The note to Leonard read:

> *I have a feeling I shall go mad. I cannot go on any longer in these terrible times. I hear voices and cannot concentrate on my work. I have fought against but cannot fight any longer. I owe all my happiness to you but cannot go on and spoil your life.*

I cannot concentrate on my work. The rain is loud, the child is very loud, we are out of milk and the cheese has a transparent, cracked look about it. Poor Virginia. It is impossible to imagine 1941. On this side of it, wars are in boxes on websites.

VIRGINIA WOOLF AND MERMAIDS

Virginia Woolf called her sister 'Vanessa Dolphin'. To Vanessa, Virginia was 'Virginia Goat'. Virginia is a river mermaid. Her nice things—her printing press, writing desk, her chairs, books, paper and ink—are as plain and secretive as a still-life painting once she is gone.

ROBIN AND ANNE AND MUSIC AND MERMAIDS

I stack *The Godwits Fly* and my three-in-one anthology of Anne books on top of each other. They are strange companions. I add my purple ukulele. They are all charms warding off the thing that would burst me into nothing. That would hang me by my mermaid hair. That would push me into the waving waves.

HANDS

In 'Wide Lovely Eyes' there is a line that compares hands with butterflies.

In the documentary, Joan Didion's hands move like ecstatic moths. Darting here, then up, then back, then out, then curl, then back.

'Mummy! Be a monster!'

WAVING

I want to ask my son if he will come and stand on the deck in the rain with me. He will be so enthusiastic, so ready, that finally, I will laugh.

When we get out there, I will notice that the lights are on in the teenage girl's room down in the greenhouse. She will stand at the window watching us. I will wave at her. My son will copy me and will wave and wave.

This essay was previously published online: https://clairemabey.substack.com/p/this-dark-country

REFERENCES

anonymous character which is baffling … Virginia Woolf, 'Women and fiction' (1929).

A very noisy evening … Sylvia Townsend Warner, *The Diaries of Sylvia Townsend Warner*, ed. Claire Harman (Virago, 1995).

ALEXIS O'CONNELL

Through the Mist and into the Sunlight

This story is about how running saved my life. It's about sweating it out when the sun warms your bare shoulders, or pressing on when the sleet stings your cheeks and the wind pushes you back. Running invigorates and imparts strength and courage to face brutal realities. Sometimes running provides the only solution to a terrifying ordeal.

With the French Foreign Legion. The beginning.

On the foggy morning of 4 October 2008, I couldn't see past the shaven heads. I needed to locate the départ banner before the gun.

'N'imagine même pas défaire les lacets de ses chaussures!'

Snickering is an international language, but John, a chivalrous British runner who had taken it upon himself to be my raceminder, translated the lieutenant's command.

'Don't even think about untying her shoelaces!'

Not another female in sight. John claimed five women had entered the race, but I couldn't see them anywhere. The women certainly wouldn't be French. Whoever they were, I was convinced they'd scarpered. All I could see were wide calf muscles and thin calf muscles, long hairy thighs and short hairy thighs, and the backs of white t-shirts—gold banded and branded légion étrangère. All the legs were eager and shuffling like one pulsating beast.

The half marathon had not been advertised for women or even the public, but a loophole disallowed denying those who dared. I was number 1431 and I couldn't quite remember how I got there. I suspected manipulation.

The race marked the end of a brutal sixteen-week training programme for the French Foreign Legion (FFL), and the 1200 men who surrounded me were the Foreign Regiment. They were competitive and feared not finishing within the qualifying time. All six companies were represented and an additional 520 military specialists. I've always thought men were on the brink between pack animals and civilisation—but when standing among so many legionnaires, I could no longer distinguish the line between running with the pack and humanity. I felt like part of a machine. A war machine. I stood straight and my biceps flexed. All my five feet six inches and 53 kilograms wanted to pack a punch. I'd sourced some aggression, maybe even some anger, or perhaps it was newly generated courage.

The race thuds alongside the steaming Canal du Midi outside the Legion's training base at Castelnaudary. I'd imagined the FFL, old-Hollywood-style in Morocco or Algeria, but Castelnaudary has housed the training base since 1976. A couple of years before the FFL's relocation to Castelnaudary, a regiment had failed to dissuade those pesky New Zealanders and their protesting navy frigates from Mururoa Atoll. French nuclear testing had been driven underground. While I'm not a heavy hitter like David Lange, who could smell uranium on anyone's breath, I regretted the lost opportunity to wear a Nuclear Free New Zealand t-shirt. Righteous indignation throbbed at my breast.

Castelnaudary sits halfway between Toulouse and Carcassonne, an area deeply bruised by centuries of horrific violence. John explained that the annual spectacle of the racing legionnaires is a way of humanising the armed men on the town perimeter.

Somewhere on the sideline stood my parents; I could hear them giggling from nervous pride as their long-haired daughter looked a bit cross and shifted in agitation among a mass of bristling soldiers. My two prepubescent sons and my wide-eyed seven-year-old daughter stared in excitement or alarm; I couldn't tell which. I'm not sure what my parents were trying to prove, but it was something.

The children's father in New Zealand was thankfully oblivious to what was going on.

To enter the race, I was certified fit by a French doctor. The Legion didn't want a 37-year-old Kiwi mother injured on their watch. What would mon Commandant say? Many of the recruits spoke less French than I did. Nevertheless, they were eerily well behaved. Their discipline appeared to be controlled by a series of hand gestures from men with big guns, and I'm not talking about their biceps.

I had thought the FFL was a specialist operations force like the British SAS or an American super soldier from the Navy Seals or Delta Force (which is so tough, it doesn't officially exist). Pre-race day, John had described them as the toughest combat warriors in the world. Their training certainly sounded unforgiving. Mine had started only two months prior, alongside the banks of the Seine and a chain of boulangeries. My three children and I were met at Charles de Gaulle by my father. We arrived, he said, pale and underweight. From that moment, we were fed love, opportunity, baguettes and cheese.

The FFL offers a new life, something not lost on me. The recruits come from all over the world. Every enlisted lieutenant's contract is five years, and he can specialise in anything from sniper to paramedic. All of them are running from somewhere, something or someone. After World War II, 60 percent of the FFL were German. No questions were asked if the SS tattoo remained unseen.

The FFL's recruitment process sets it apart from every other combat force in the world. Only men between seventeen and a half and thirty-nine and a half can enter. If an applicant is wanted by Interpol for murder or drug trafficking, the FFL doesn't want them. Otherwise, for any youthful man who can make it to one of the recruitment centres in France (which are open 24/7), the FFL will immediately take care of their accommodation, food, clothing and healthcare, free of charge. Identity documents or even admitting to a name is voluntary. A recruit could be unskilled, a criminal or even married, but if they pass selection and serve, they'll be naturalised as a French citizen. After three years of honourable service, they can be 'rectified', which means their new 'real identity' is issued. All legionnaires are recorded as single. The FFL has never been short of recruitment hopefuls, but they can be disqualified if they have too many missing teeth, unstable knees, or they're missing a finger.

Richard Stockton, a science and technology writer from Sacramento, claims the FFL fatality rate has climbed as high as 70 percent, and he compares the FFL unfavourably to Texas's death row. But he conflates time periods for effect. In recent years, the FFL's horrific training exercises have caused more deaths than combat. To be a legionnaire is perilous. For a legion of runaways, the Code of Honour is ironic: *never abandon your dead, your wounded, or your arms.* I pictured the Ukraine-born legionnaire recently blown to bits by an improvised explosive device (IED) in Mali and wondered whether any unexpected obstacles were planned for the race.

My sons had always loved the Marx Brothers, so while we were in France, their grandfather introduced them to Laurel and Hardy and Abbott and Costello. The boys acquired a new way of seeing the world. In *The Flying Deuces* (1939), Ollie falls in unrequited love and an opportunistic FFL officer promises a solution. Stan and Ollie enlist in the Legion, but their exploits make a mockery of the constant marching, the mountains of laundry and ironing, and the idiotic exercise of jockeying for masculine dominance. Stan and Ollie attempt to desert. They are caught and thrown in prison to be shot at sunrise. At this point, my sons' stomachs are aching from all the hilarity. Stan and Ollie's attempt to escape is predictably shambolic and futile. Their aerial getaway is foiled by a band of pesky pigeons: Europe's rats of the sky. I can still hear my eldest son's uncontrollable hyperventilating laughter when the dead Ollie rises to heaven on angel wings and returns as a horse sporting the Ollie moustache. Ollie had wished to be a horse rather than suffer unrequited love, and God had blessed him with what he most desired.

In *Abbott & Costello in the Foreign Legion* (1950), Bud and Lou are put in danger by an untrustworthy woman (there's a theme here) and tricked into signing the Legion's five-year contract. They innocently believed free room and board was on offer without repercussion. Instead, they found themselves at the mercy of a lieutenant with a German accent. I'm not sure what my sons were expecting the morning their mother joined the Legion line-up, but it was something between slapstick and a comedic tragedy. I was beginning to wonder whether a woman was to blame for every perplexing FFL story.

The children and I were in France because my parents had a long-term agreement to look after a thirteenth-century (1210) château owned by an American banker and his wife. Despite the Global Financial Crisis, the château remained secure even when the homes of thousands of former American customers were not. Our American banker was a good guy; he became part of the GFC rebuild and could only use the château three weeks a year. Kiwi contacts live in the château the rest of the year, so the freestanding armour remains polished and the bathtub clear of pigeons. Fortunately for us, my retired parents were reliable château caretakers and extended family had proven past favourites. My father discovered Blanquette de Limoux (the first French bubbles) and reacquainted himself with the language—in that order, I believe. My mother found a shabby-chic fashion label to sell exclusively in New Zealand.

The children had begun to relax. In the château's village, my younger son, now considerably less anxious, managed to ride a bike. Back in New Zealand, he'd been told he never would. He caught lizards and collected medieval figurines from La Cité. He acted out uninhibited make-believe for hours. My oldest son revelled in the possibilities of new freedoms. His awakened mind placed him on the edge of imaginative combustion. He asked for things with confidence. My daughter clung to her gentle grandfather and found a turreted fairy castle at the source of the Canal du Midi in the Black Mountains. Her eyes progressed from reflective mirror-glass to a clearing mist. We encountered a large and angry ladder snake. I saved the day by backing everyone slowly away. The faces of fearful children began to glow.

I discovered hours of vineyards, fields of rapeseed, the Abbaye Sainte-Marie de Villelongue, an old Roman bridge, and a cross where a member of the French Resistance had been shot in the back. I ran in the sun until the bats chased me back. I ran in the rain, slapping my running shoes on the backs of tiny snakes that were everywhere underfoot. I ran all the way up to Saissac and back down through Saint-Martin, and I ran on Wednesdays, which was hunt day. The hunters kept a close eye out. I praised their dead boar.

In France, all cemeteries must provide clean and accessible drinking water, and because cemeteries lie on the edge of every village, I was never thirsty. I ran past the crosses through the morning mist and into the sunlight. I never thought about where the water came from or how the dead filtered it—the water always tasted like heaven. French women in the south don't run, so for a few months, I was an oddity. The squarish French farmers considered me eccentric and guided me over their land in bemused confusion, more *oh là là* than the English *ooh la la*. I repeated my running, what some would claim a gruelling freedom, and I gained muscle.

The château has a squared turret covered in ivy that can be reached through a trapdoor, and a garden that springs from the bones of Visigoths. There are barred dungeon rooms my parents renovated into an enormous wine cellar. There's a swimming pool I remember dappled in sunlight where my nervous children learnt to swim, and a playground that failed to hold their attention because everywhere else was too fantastic. The wonderland would change anyone's life, but for my children, their whole world unfurled. I didn't understand at the time, but our initial appearance in Paris, though not entirely unexpected, was heartbreaking for my parents. They were fearful for our future and their hope for our French experience was not one-dimensional. Our unstable situation was not a secret. Volatile secrets are hard to hide.

At night inside the château's blue bedroom, I would hear the legionnaires march past—completely silent, except for the thud thud of their boots. A group of broken and invisible outcasts, exorcising their past and attempting to latch onto an alternative expression of honour.

It wouldn't be true to say that I had fallen out of love. Any sort of nuanced feeling was a luxury. For fourteen years, my focus had been to withstand each day. I'd become disassociated from my nerve endings. My body knew danger and wore it on the surface, and my mind was crushed by close calls, confusion and the unpredictability of instability. But my situation was not only my situation. I had three young children who had seen too much. No mother, if she can help it, should allow her children to be subjected as I had. In a sense, I was a wounded soldier. I needed extracting from a battlefield. Someone had noted that my first instinct, when I felt the children were safe, was to run, and that I looked and behaved better for it. That same someone had come up with the bonkers idea that running with the FFL would give me the strength to face my plight. The message was silent but not subtle. The children's excited expressions at the mere thought of their mother running with the FFL gave me no choice.

I'd absorbed from my church background that running from a marriage was a cowardly thing to do. You ran from sin, specifically sexual sin, but you didn't run from marriage. Sometimes, even often, immediate circumstances surge beyond idealism and to run is the only courageous and intelligent response. While I didn't untangle the complexities in France, my parents' posting at the château provided the space to experience another feeling, and to breathe. We had become increasingly isolated in New Zealand. Friends and extended family had been rigidly discouraged. I thought I'd simply embraced a wonderful holiday opportunity for the children and their grandparents, but in retrospect, our few months in France proved to be our départ banner.

The half marathon with the legionnaires would become my first significant running experience of many. John, a friend of my parents, coached me all the way; after months of training, my body plodded strongly like a metronome. Every kilometre was a sub-five-minute kilometre. I didn't embarrass my sex, although I managed to embarrass a large proportion of the legionnaires that morning. If the FFL took women, they would have taken me. My teeth are sound and I'm not missing any fingers. My children ran with me for the last 100 metres, and a line of FFL soldiers clapped and cheered us to the arrivée. I felt beautiful, strong and capable. It was the sort of liberation I desperately wanted.

While I had been training, my sons began to ooze energy and enthusiasm for history. To them, the Languedoc was a blockbuster—the land of the jaw-dropping cave paintings—the real Astérix and Obélix, and even Hannibal, who passed through on his way to Rome. The bones of Vandals were resurrected and the Saracens were expelled by Charlemagne's knights. Our château (we still call it 'ours') was built at the height of the Albigensian Crusade. The Crusade may have lost its passion had it not been for the fanatical Simon de Montfort (1175–1218). The Cathars, sometimes called the Good Christians, believed in an odd mix of Catholicism, Gnosticism and Platonism, but they were non-aggressors and community focused. Nevertheless, they were declared 'heretics' and a military campaign was ordered by the Roman Catholic Church (Pope Innocent III, 1160–1216). The Cathars were to be erased from Occitania.

The village of Bram, which possessed the closest boulangerie to our château, was the centre of Cathar belief in 1209. Simon de Montfort and his knights surrounded the town and trapped one hundred villagers seeking refuge inside the church. He ordered their top lips, noses, and ears cut off, and then he gouged their eyes out. One Cathar was allowed to keep one eye so he could lead the survivors away and spread panic throughout the Languedoc. The remaining Cathars fled to Montségur.

Eight hundred years later, the children and I followed. We sat on the ruins of the last Cathar fortress, watched the autumn leaves fall, and stared at the earth where the last Cathar women and children were burnt. We've loved the Occitan cross ever since. Simon de Montfort crushed the Cathars into non-existence and became a hero. We thought him a coward. Sometimes horrifying stories come to a satisfying conclusion. Simon de Montfort was killed at the siege of Toulouse in June 1218. He was hit on the head by a stone, apparently from one of the siege engines operated by women. Another story, probably apocryphal, had Simon de Montfort killed by a woman who dropped a stone on his head from the wall above. Either way, his death reads delightfully. Of course, the boys loved the grotesquerie.

On our return to New Zealand, I left the marital home. I took the children, the photos of our time in France and the poster for the Legion's half marathon that my father proudly ripped from the window of a Castelnaudary tobacconist. I can barely comprehend our growth. Of course, the 'what ifs' and the 'could've happened' are speculative and debatable but I believe, and time has proven, that running with the FFL saved my life—possibly even the lives of my children—and certainly our health and imaginations. Through the mist and into the sunlight.

I have not stopped running. I've run half marathons, marathons and ultra-marathons. I accidentally won the Oparara Wilderness Trail Run (32km). Age-group winning has happened because I've got older, and the number of competitors has reduced to equal the podium levels. My favourite races are the Kepler Challenge (60km) and the Routeburn Classic (32km). I'm not fast or competitive. I run like a metronome. I run with joy. Since the FFL, I've run through Tuscan hills and over the cobblestones of La Rambla. I've run through Provence and the Alpes-Côte d'Azur. The Port Hills have carried me through my toughest days. In their own way, the children learned to run as well. The strength of their imaginations remains their strongest distinguishing characteristic. There is a tragic story here, but it is not ours.

Some years of running later, I met another runner. A runner who always let me win. He ran with me on our honeymoon, at least for the first 20km. I had to run back to our rented cottage, grab water, and run it back to him. He joined the New York Running Club to make me happy. He ran the Grete Waitz race around Central Park to keep me company. After promising to run with him, I ditched him at the start line and beat him by ten minutes. Red in the face and exhausted, he celebrated my success. I pay him back with laughter. One of our favourite runs was through the vineyards above the Cinque Terre in 2019—

my husband's face still as red as Chianti. I took photos for evidence. As we climbed above the vines and olive trees we encountered an unexpected obstacle. I had time to yell 'snake' but not 'dead snake'. My husband ran the fastest I've ever seen him run—but on the spot—yelping on the back of the dead snake. A moment of pure joy. I still break out in spontaneous uncontrollable laughter when I think about it.

REFERENCE
claims the FFL fatality rate … Richard Stockton, 'Run away with the foreign legion', *All That's Interesting*, 5 February 2015: https://allthatsinteresting.com/foreign-legion-history

Pig Love Slop

I began attending auctions religiously, finding the ritual of it soothing. I'd found a room where objects and belongings rushed in and out like a tide. As if the world's possessions were an ocean, and I could muck about in one bit of muddy estuary.

*

Sighs, the rhythms of our heartbeats, contractions of childbirth, orgasms, all flow into time just as pendulum clocks placed next to one another soon beat in unison.
—Lucia Berlin

*

'I'm worried you're a hoarder,' my mum told me as she moved my things into my new house. Thiss was a gross exaggeration; it wasn't that bad, just a few old pairs of shoes with the leather scuffed and worn; yellowed pillows, stiff from old age; paperbacks with torn covers and mildewed edges; a box of kitchen utensils I'd bought from an auction. I knew what most of the things were, knew where they went, though some strange appliances sifted around in kitchen drawers catching dust.

*

For my birthday, my friends give me a copy of *A Manual for Cleaning Women* by Lucia Berlin. 'Wait,' I say, confused, 'why are the women being cleaned?'

*

In my university paper about memory, we learn that most memory problems are not an issue with retrieval, but with storage. In other words: if you weren't there to experience the thing in the first place, for example, due to dissociation or stress or distraction, then there's no trace left behind to be remembered.

*

The problem with a numbered list, my writing supervisor, Pip, says, *is that it implies a forward motion. It makes it harder to return to prior threads of the narrative.*

*

There are no comfortable chairs in my house growing up, not a one. The dinner table is a long and narrow wooden thing, a wide and dark stained piece of wood in the heart of the kitchen, two hard upright seats at each head, and backless pews along the sides.

I do my Kumon homework at this table, maths problems that centre on repetition, learning through a sequential memorisation process of addition, subtraction, multiplication, division.

My writing has a troublesome way of etching into the table's waxy surface. When I look down at dinner I can see the faint lines of my working, the answer reached plus the steps of how I got there.

*

On one of my stories, my writing teacher Elaine notes: 'I prefer my writers (and psychologists) to have the aura of magicians about them, and not show how the trick is done ...'

*

I pluck a book from the shelf in my hall, Mary Oliver's *New and Selected Poems*. I take it upstairs, lie in bed with it next to Sean. 'Can I read you a poem?' I ask.

'Sure.' He sounds tired.

I open it and on the inside cover is a handwritten note from my dad. Blue biro, his writing an elegant slant, angled against the page. I scroll my eyes through the contents, separated out into time periods, the various volumes of Oliver's work.

I scan the titles, searching for a bird poem in the hope Sean might like it because Sean likes birds. 'Wait, she's got a poem called "Egret" and then another called "The Egrets"? Can you do that? Name two poems the same thing? I can't pick a poem. You choose.'

I pass Sean the book and he thumbs along the pages until it catches and falls open.

'Let me see!' I say, peering over at what he's found. 'Egret' it reads at the top of the page. I make witchy fingers at him and a 'wooooo' sound.

'Stop that,' he says.

*

My mum can't sleep without earplugs, and she keeps them in a little paua shell next to her bed, bullets of orange foam that she uses to block her ears. She has trouble throwing the old ones away, so it's a graveyard of them, a pile of silence she's accumulated over the years.

Every afternoon, she takes a nap. She did this when my brother and I were kids, corralling us into a circle of her words while speaking in a Very Firm Voice: 'No noise. I am lowering the Cone of Silence!'

The Cone of Silence was never to be lifted, it was a precious and sacred thing from which no sound could escape. A bell jar for naptime, impenetrable, and we were all stuck inside of it for the next thirty minutes while she dozed. We crept around the house. It was always so tempting to shatter the glass, but I knew it wasn't worth it. I tried to pipe down.

*

I've always thought I'd be a good plumber. I take a secret pleasure in the blockage of a sink, the knowledge that my skills will soon come in handy. I wrap my hands around the thick white pipes and then twist the sturdy plastic loose. I place a bucket underneath to catch any overflow, and then reach my hand in, turning one end of me into a small white claw, scratching at the insides to dislodge gunk which I shake into the bucket's wide green mouth waiting patiently where I've placed it.

*

I deliver a training programme to district court staff on behalf of a sexual violence prevention NGO. The training is called 'Recognise, Respond, Refer'. I'm flown to Christchurch and put up in a hotel. The room I'm in is very small, with a mirror entirely filling one wall next to the bed. It's a very modern set-up and reminds me of those public toilets that play songs as you pee—usually a cheery piano rendition of 'What the World Needs Now Is Love Sweet Love'.

The hotel room is too smart for its own good, with a control panel next to the door that's difficult to operate. Though I press the 'bedtime' setting, a light above my head turns on at half-hour intervals throughout the night. Each time, I roll over with a groan to press a series of buttons, a complex Morse code, trying to shut it off. Then I go back to sleep.

*

I present my clean laundry like evidence, the tangled mess of it in the rattan basket that lives in the hallway outside my bedroom. The handle's fallen off, but it's still good, carrying the bits okay if I keep my arms hugged around it tight enough. After the handle falls off it, I think: *well, guess that's it then*, but more bits of wicker continue to flick off and I find them in the laundry closet, sitting on top of the washer. 'How'd you get in here?' I ask the thing, frowning at it with my hands stuck on my hips in disapproval.

*

I start to notice that my classmates' stories have affect contained in them, emotions I can feel while reading their words. Perhaps I am occupying their minds, or maybe holding a small animal part of them in my palms.

'This story feels a little numb,' I announce, or, 'I love how much energy's here; it's really coming off the page.'

I start to doubt myself, wondering what I'm projecting onto the work and what's actually there. I know there isn't any true way to separate the two. I often have the feeling that something else is trying to get through the words, another story lying underneath in wait, hoping to be discovered. I share this thought, then wonder if it's wanted. *What's reflection and what's projection?* I think, gazing around me, the once solid world starting to waver.

*

Elaine tells me to choose either italics or quote marks for speech, not to use both. *But what if I want to use italics to suggest a more internal speech and quote marks to be more external?*

'Pick one,' she says.

*

My friends Matthew and Gus make up a game in which two objects are introduced and you pick which one you are. The original choice was 'olive oil or sea salt' but it's moved far beyond that now. After you pick, everyone else gets to weigh in, which sometimes results in strange debates.

'You are *not* smoked salmon,' I laugh at Gus, rolling my eyes. 'You're cream cheese through and through!'

It's fun to show someone how ignorant they can be to themselves. Who do they think they are, claiming to be a rattan wastepaper basket when they are so clearly an industrial-sized paper shredder?

*

I take one of my assessment reports to my clinical psychology supervisor. I've used the term 'true self' and she questions me on it: 'Can you explain to me what you mean by that here?'

I find it difficult to articulate and she gently suggests I not use psychoanalytic terms that I don't understand.

*

I stay at my mother's place for the weekend, and she says if I help her clean out her closet she'll give me any clothes she gets rid of that I want. The thought of organising someone else's shit is weirdly enticing, and I agree, standing on a stepladder in the darkened length of it, reaching towards eighties sweaters and holding them up to decide which pile to throw them into.

'But what if I want that later and I no longer have it?' she worries, citing an old boyfriend's jacket that she threw away forty years ago as a terrifying reminder that a thing, once discarded, is gone. I groan and try to convince her to loosen her grip a bit, hoping we might make the giveaway pile larger, reducing the strain on the already precarious stack of keeps.

*

I am watching the trailer for *Memento*; it resonates. I stare open-mouthed at the screen while my right hand blindly takes another sesame cracker, freeing it from flimsy plastic. I go to dip it in my hummus and see another cracker already sitting there. Right where some part of me left it. I laugh and look around, but there's nobody there.

*

I find a Post-it note that I tucked away in a drawer, a scrawl of black pen on dark pink. It reads: 'Childhood is a land I cannot return to; I am homesick for it.'

*

'Writing isn't therapy, Maggie,' Elaine says gently, then hands me a stapled print-out; a *Guardian* article with a smiling woman on the cover, an author who's written a 500-word essay saying the same thing.

*

'Your mind works in mysterious ways,' my high school geometry teacher, Mrs Aarons, tells me, shaking her head.

Mrs Aarons has Bell's palsy, and half her face is drooped on one side. She's slicked it with clear lubricant to keep her eye moist as it no longer produces tears. She is a strange woman with a small family—a husband and a blonde, surly toddler I don't like.

Also, there's a strange smell to her, a savoury scent that wafts from the end of the hall, infiltrating the entryways of the rooms nearby.

*

I clean the garlic press last, knowing it will reek, and it does. I scrape the thick heel of indented vegetal peel free with my fingernails and then poke through the press's silver holes with a dish brush.

After, I'm infiltrated, my skin a porous border for the stench. I stink even after a shower, my skin red and raw from scrubbing at myself. I bring my fingers to my nose. Still there. I can't wash it off.

*

I'm standing at the whiteboard of the courthouse, marker pen poised. 'Okay, so what are some signs a person might have experienced trauma?' The group quickly gets the most common ones: feeling fearful, not leaving the house much, isolating from friends and family, alcohol and drug use. I smile and nod, affirming all the answers, repeating them back so each person knows they've been heard.

'What about dissociation, like things don't really feel real,' a goateed man offers.

'Yep!' I mumble dissociation under my breath as I scrawl it on the board.

A middle-aged white woman raises her hand: 'What about cleaning a lot? OCD-type stuff?'

I pause, holding the dry end of the pen to my lips. 'Hmmmm, I'm actually not so sure about that one. I haven't heard of that before.'

*

Friday night sees me with a yellow Chux cloth in one hand while the other presses play on a podcast I've recently discovered: *Tuesday Toolbox ACA*, which is an adult child of alcoholics recovery group that meets weekly in Cobble Hill, Brooklyn.

Each episode opens with a few bars of clangy piano riff and then the voice of Ann, who describes herself as 'a Tuesday Toolbox member and an adult child'. She speaks in a soft sing-song voice, which makes it sound as though she is herself a child, but also an adult speaking gently to that very same child.

I am cleaning the back doors that lead into the garden because I want to be able to see the green. As I remove the dust and muck, the white paint begins to chip away. I have to be gentle, to try and clean without removing too much as the wood's already leaking and when rain comes in hard from the side a thin line of wet sits at the lip of the window. Sometimes I have to take a towel to it, wiping the moisture away.

*

She steps into the dark swamp
where the long wait ends.—Mary Oliver

*

'Just make sure that the anger doesn't do the writing,' Elaine says to me one afternoon in her office. I'm trying to stay with the conversation, but I've had a migraine all day, and the window behind her seems too big. Looking out of it feels like pressing on a bruise.

'Why? What happens if I write from my anger?'

'A person can lose track of the deeper story.'

*

My classmate brings in a poem by a writer they admire. It's written entirely in computer programming code. *Someone* has bothered me and I'm crawling out of my skin not saying the goddamned thing. The poets discuss the piece thoughtfully, offering possible meanings one morsel at a time like unhungry monks. I want to bite off the poem's legs. I want to spit bloody code from my mouth. A poet speaks and the other poets nod. I can't hear over the ringing in my ears. *Can't someone in this room be honest for once? Can't someone just say what they fucking think? Do I have to tell everyone that I love everything? Do I have to tell everyone that I love them?*

I don't say any of this. Instead, I fill my chest with air like a proud bird and say: 'Could I put a potato on the table and call that a poem. Huh?'

The walk home is a shameful walk, a dog leading itself to the pound, head down and eyes looking dolefully up. Part of me wants to sink like shit into the bowels of the earth, but instead I puff myself up hot and full of air. My steps are getting pouty.

'But that was a *bad* poem,' I say to my friend as we walk down the hill.

I tell Sean about it later, trying to pass it off like it's funny. He laughs, but there's a nervous edge to it, like maybe I've fallen over the lip of something. Gone too far.

*

'Memory can be thought of like a filing cabinet,' I say to the attendees in the courtroom. I'm nervous but my voice strides ahead of me. 'When something traumatic happens, it's like the cabinet's been tipped over, and all of the files get scattered across the floor. A therapist's job is to help the client put the memories back in order.' I pause and give a little smile. 'Now obviously, that is not your job and we aren't asking you to do that. But this is just to give some idea of why a customer you're dealing with might be a little erratic, or seem confused, or agitated.'

I think I've said this okay, but it doesn't quite make sense even though I know the words off by heart. The metaphor keeps getting jumbled in my mind.

*

I'm very literal, I tell the poets in apology. Elaine has asked what the washing machine image in someone's poem means and I say 'washing machine.' It just blurts out of my mouth I can't stop it.

*

I do laundry like it's breathing. Cycling it in and out and in and out, quietly opening the door to the laundry cupboard to check on it as it spins round and round, the frothy bubbles a reminder that it's not done. I'll come check on it later, I say to myself. *Don't forget!*

*

When asked if she likes something, my mother says: 'Do a pig love *slop!*' Her words are thrown out with dramatic relish, the roof of her mouth happy to usher the syllables out.

*

> *And forever those nights snarl*
> *the delicate machinery of the days.* —Mary Oliver

*

I play a game at Matthew and Gus's place where we all go round and share a saying our mothers used to say, something that doesn't make any sense outside

the language of our family. I choose: *It doesn't make my socks roll up and down.*
It reminds me of the Wicked Witch of the West, her striped socks curling her
up beneath the fallen house til there's no trace of her left.

*

I locate the little girl's shoe, tired and brown and weathered, in the top drawer
inside the laundry cupboard. *I think this belongs with the house*, the prior
owners wrote in their handwritten note.

It's right where I put it, under a toolkit and series of screwdrivers—Phillips
head, flat, and square. The shoe's very dusty, shrivelled, with a little button
on the side, receded into the rest of the leather. It is disgusting. I must rid my
architecture of all foreign bodies. *Perhaps, I think, this is an opportunity!* I
must give the shoe as a sacrificial offering to whatever wrathful whatever I've
whatevered.

*

My mum's got a stuffed animal that she keeps on her bed. She's had it since she
was a kid, a folksy little pig sewn in a thick pink fabric. The pig's wearing wide-
wale green corduroy overalls. It's getting a little old and frayed nowadays but it
still goes. It's still good.

*

It's cumbersome, moving the shoe with one hand while holding the stick of
burning sage with the other, a steady stream of smoke wisping into the cobwebs
that line the ceiling of the laundry cupboard. It's under the stairs, so the ceiling
slants down at the same angle I ascend to bed each evening.

I take the shoe into the kitchen where the vibes are better, place it on the floor
over the spot where I've heard the rat scratching. *Only god lives here, only god
lives here*, I say, circling the sage round the shoe some multiple of times until I
am some semblance of satisfied. I walk with my items— shoe, sage, and lighter
(the sage needs to be continually reignited with a flick of tiny silver wheel)—
outside and can hear my neighbours playing dubstep two doors over, low male
voices rumbling in non-conversation. I can practically hear the slurps of beer.

*

'Your right eye is almost perfect,' my OkCupid date tells me. We are sitting at a
picnic table outside a café in Berlin and he seems disappointed that I've ordered

orange soda and not a lager. 'The right side is your masculine side. But,' he pauses to peer at me, 'your left eye is drooping slightly. This is the feminine side. She looks a little sad.'

*

Now I feel uncertain. Where is the best place to put a cursed child's shoe of yore? The leather has shrivelled up so much that the sole of the thing sticks out beyond the upper, which has receded like a gingivitis-ridden gum. I am desperate to throw it over the fence into the back of the preschool. There is some symmetry to this, and my gut tells me *yes, do it*. But what if it lands on the roof? In many ways a good outcome: out of reach of small, jammy hands. But also bad: from that vantage, perhaps it could rain evil down. Surely corrugated iron would not serve as a proper shield?

There is nowhere to hide it out here, the back fence erected proud and strong with not a nook nor cranny to be seen along its length. The side fence is a little shoddier, and I opt for tucking it under. There, it sits in a corner and I pray a quiet apology under my breath to the neighbour: *sorry, sorry, I'll come back for it, promise*!

*

I message Matthew and Gus to ask what they call the game, the one where you pick the thing that you are. Now I know not to trust my own memory. Matthew writes: We call it '*Each to their own*.' And also '*To each their own*.' Pretty interchangeably. He says they've been playing a lot lately and poses me one: astrology or astronomy?

*

It's been a long time since I've cleaned the bathroom mirror and white dots of toothpaste are splattered all over it. I can only see myself through the stars, like I'm flying through space, the mirrored version of that old screensaver we used to have on the desktop in Dad's office. Only now I can see myself in the solar system, my milky face hovering in the way.

*

I watch a YouTube clip of Oprah talking to her life coach, Martha Beck. Beck reminds me of a Muppet, her smile so broad and available it looks like her head might hinge right back so a song can spill out. Beck tells Oprah that the best way to do a psychological self-portrait is to think of the room in your house that you would least like someone to see, and then use three words to describe it. I immediately think of my closet. *Messy, dirty, shameful.*

I tell Sean about the video. 'It's kinda like the house is a body. So if that's the case, what do you think my closet represents?' It's a rhetorical question, what Oprah might call a 'teachable moment'.

Sean grins. 'Is it your asshole?'

'*No,*' I say, exasperated, 'obviously it's my heart.'

*

My haul from Mum's closet is pretty good; a long corduroy skirt that makes me feel like a Mormon who's started listening to Shirley Manson, and a lilac turtleneck that I'm on the fence about but decide to take. But the best bit is the sweatshirt, blue and faded, soft from wear. On the front is a diagram of an artificial heart in shades of white. It depicts the heart itself, and then a row of stitches across it, discs and wires stuck in the three valves and sans-serif lettering that reads 'JARVIK-7™'. Centred on the back are two lines of text, bold and blocky capitals, followed by a mysterious ellipsis:

> *AND THE BEAT*
> *GOES ON ...*

*

I read Sean another Mary Oliver poem: 'Picking Blueberries, Austerlitz, New York, 1957.' It concludes: 'rising out of the rough weeds, listening and looking. Beautiful girl, where are you?'

'What do you think the poem is about?' I ask, his arms around me.

He smiles, 'Picking blueberries, I guess.'

*

I snap half a sleeping pill and put it in my mouth. I take a swig of water, then turn out the light.

SUSAN WARDELL

Mary, Me and the Bees: In search of the good settler

When I feel unsettled, I go out into the garden and stand on the piece of land that bears my name. I watch my small black-and-white cat stalk the fat fidgety tauhou. I see birds come to both the kōwhai and the rowan. I learn the names of plants and look for signs—for a map—of how to live in this place as tangata Tiriti. Then I get out my spade, and I dig till I ache.

I had been searching for the good settler a long time, and then in sailed Mary with her two skeps of bees.

Part One: Mary

It is easier for everyone if the good settler is a woman. Even better if she has soft ringlets, rosy cheeks, and is the first at something brave or useful. Mary Bumby was the first person to bring honeybees to New Zealand. Born in a Yorkshire market town set between two medieval roads, she grew up surrounded by green fields. On the cover of an airport paperback, she would be *The Butcher's Daughter*. The sequel would be *The Missionary's Sister*, featuring the story of her daring decision to accompany her brother John on a voyage across the ocean in 1838. John was to take up a position as superintendent of a Wesleyan Methodist mission station. Mary was twenty-seven years old and grieved leaving her childhood home, her ageing father. She worried about her brother's health in the cramped conditions on the vessel—a small wooden sailing ship called *The James*, with fifty-six people on board—twenty-one of whom were missionaries and their families.

For five months, passengers with hands as pale as bible leaf tended each other in their wooden frames, amid cockroaches and changeable weather. The ritual motions of their mouths in prayer marked the distant inflorescence of hope that was their destination: *New Zealand*. It was dark in the hold below, where Mary tended her own hopes. Her brother had a taste for honey, and in service of this, she had loaded two straw baskets—called 'skeps'—aboard the ship in England. As they sailed, these down-facing baskets rested on a board inside a box, carefully insulated and ventilated. Inside them, several thousand British black bees (*Apis mellifera*) slept in a simulated winter. For months, amidst her intense seasickness, Mary regularly descended to feed them with sugar water. When the sun emerged between storm skies, she carried them up to the deck. You can imagine them, can't you? The bees, emerging in a maelstrom of confusion, under her watchful eye and the crew's bemused stares—whirling in circles, trying to orient themselves to their strange surroundings. After circling enough times to memorise the position of the hive entrance, they spread out on a 'cleaning flight' that mimicked their standard seasonal habits. But something about water disorients bees. Finding salt on all sides, they inevitably wobbled back to the ship in bewilderment. And so, the whole ship slept with dreams that buzzed.

*

The good settler needs somewhere to settle. On the south bank of Hokianga Harbour, near the Ngāpuhi village of Horeke, was the Māngungu mission station. Twelve years prior, chief Eruera Maihi Patuone had given the Wesleyans permission to set up a station there. The station's founder, the Reverend John Hobbs, carefully designed a Georgian-style house to stand at its centre. Over the years that followed, outbuildings and a school sprang up, and gardens and an orchard were planted around them. Such efforts, to sculpt this new land into the image of paradise—which is to say, the image of England.

Mary set up her hives in the churchyard—a spot chosen to keep them away from 'the curiosity of the Maoris'. From here, the bees emerged to explore, over golden sand and golden tussock, into bush with boughs constantly swinging under bird worship. They soon settled to the task of tonguing native church bells and the pinched yellow faces of English weeds. When winter came again, it was less salty but just as wet. John travelled the surrounding countryside, visiting other missionaries, while Mary kept house as planned. By spring, the surrounding mānuka (*Leptospermum scoparium*) was in full bloom, and the bees set ecstatically to work again. The first honey harvest would have been complete early the following year. Just in time for the arrival of their most auspicious guests.

*

It was 1840, and Te Tiriti had just been signed at Waitangi—on the opposite side of this crest of the North Island. It was brought to Māngungu on 12 February. John was away again when the Ngāpuhi chiefs arrived—seventy of them, all men of wealth and status—along with Lieutenant Governor William Hobson representing the Crown. Three thousand others gathered outside as witnesses. You can imagine it, can't you? Mary opening the front door, welcoming inside the chosen few; the harbour behind them vast and shining. Mary in the kitchen, taking the first fruits of her labour and drizzling gold syrup onto chunks of bread to present to her guests—an unexpected sweetness for a serious matter.

Aotearoa already had bees, of course. At least twenty-eight different native varieties remain. But those species nest alone and none make honey, so perhaps the chiefs, as they milled around the station, puzzled at the mystery of insects that were happy to be boxed, happy not to notice what was being stolen. Perhaps their secretions made the colonists seem sweeter, almost like good settlers, in their labours to serve a hidden queen, to build an empire shared on bread. Or perhaps they knew better.

The guests left with history inked into place—poorly translated, a promise to be stretched and sold for 180 years and counting. Governor Hobson and his wife Eliza had obtained their own hives within the year. John came back, but in June, he departed again on a small vessel that had just deposited the Reverend Gideon Smales, another Yorkshire man and minister, who offered Mary 'heart and hand' the very next month. She declined, too busy worrying about her brother's waning health. When John was late to return, she woke in the night to the sound of his voice calling her name—glimpsed him in the doorway for just a second, and then gone. A letter finally broke her vigil, bearing the news that his boat had been upturned taking a shortcut across the Hauraki Gulf. Dark tentacles of grief took hold; her mind was raked by images of John 'sleeping in the cold and greedy sea.' The Reverend Smales set out with the station's founder, the Reverend Hobbs, to try and retrieve his body, but ultimately failed. He proposed a second time a few months later, and she accepted.

*

It is easier for everyone if the good settler loves children. Mary and Gideon tended the hives. Mary sent chunks of honeycomb out to other settler families, solidifying lifelong memories among the children of their very first taste of honey. They kept notes on the amount of honey and the number of swarms. By 1843, along with two sons, they had five colonies of bees. Each colony was named after a different British royal.

Meanwhile, Reverend Hobbs had fallen out with the other missionaries, recording his special disapproval of Gideon Smales, who, he opined, spent too much time helping his wife with the gardening and the bees when he should have been out converting Māori. The truth was that Gideon and Mary had become increasingly worried about the actions of the New Zealand Company and its links to the growing exploitation of Māori. They moved away from Māngungu, taking their hives with them.

For a while, Mary and the children were left in Nelson, while Gideon tried to insert himself into tense arguments over land in Porirua. Later, they moved to Aotea Great Barrier Island together and had four more children. By that time, several other people had successfully brought bees from England, settling them into various parts of the country, many unaware of Mary's stock. Over time they argued over who had been first—over who would be remembered as the 'father' of beekeeping in New Zealand—leaving Mary a woman-shaped footnote in the nation's history. How many of today's honeybees are her descendants?

Part Two: Me

I had been searching for the good settler for a long time, and then in drove the truck with my two boxes of bees.

It was easier for me to be at peace with my Pākehā identity once I could say that I tended the earth. My patch of earth rises beside the silver banner of the harbour in Ōtepoti Dunedin—a region in Te Wai Pounamu belonging to Kāi Tahu. It is here I learned to get my hands dirty. But I hadn't been a gardener for long when I became enamoured of the fuzzy, relentless workers that tended the flowers alongside me. They were romantic, yes, but also productive. After some investigations, I decided to pay a company to rent some hives. A few weeks later, a white man arrived in a white truck with boxes of bees strapped on the back. Several crushed bees were stuck under the straps, I noticed, with pity. I didn't yet know how readily bees die.

We chose a spot at the top of the garden just across from my vegetable patch, and then he turned the valve to let them free. Without a suit, I was forced to stand back—but stayed close enough to watch them begin to whirl. They were soon a cloud of energy—not so much angry as determined. It was quite a sight, but I felt a deep sense of relief when they eventually settled. My bees. Gentle bees, I was promised, and if they showed signs of developing a more aggressive culture, I could call and ask for the hive to be swapped out. I wondered how I would feel if my bees were replaced with others—not identifiably different, but not mine.

That night, after darkness fell, I opened my back door, walked past the overflowing recycling bins and up the steps beside the pink-flowering mānuka. Across the water, I could see the lives of strangers glowing amber and gold along the dark hills. Further up, I stopped and lowered myself onto the bark chips under a hulking blackcurrant bush. From a pool of deep shadow, I watched the clouds and the moon slide over each other, as if neither were really there. Then, carefully, I turned onto my hands and knees and leaned forward to place an ear against the hive.

A sleeping beehive sounds like a distant ocean. Low and soft, a roar, but far away. You can imagine it, can't you? Placing your palm against the painted wood, feeling its vibrations. Some people say you should see the hive as the organism, not the individual bee. Bees sleep in shifts, individually or in groups, using empty wax cells as bed chambers or gathering at the quiet edges. Some hold onto each other's legs. The foragers, especially, sleep at night, so they can resume activity the next day. Others must stay awake to fan the hive, to evaporate the water from the day's nectar. They clean the hive and keep the brood warm. Their activity nested in my ear like the sound of the universe boxed and sleeping. Eventually, I had to return to the electric glow of the wooden villa below and my husband preparing the children for bed.

*

When my children were small, I often filled long afternoons with museums. Armed with snacks and nappies, we would trail around Toitū—formerly the Dunedin Early Settlers' Museum—poking fingers into corners of the past that were not quite our own. Their favourite spot was the replica ship's cabin where, in dim light between piles of luggage, invisible wires channel the moan of strained planks and work to make your ears into vessels of history. 'Put me to bed, Mama!' the kids would giggle, tucking themselves under the rough blankets on the wooden bunks. Around the corner, screens told stories of fever and the death of infants aboard, and I didn't know how to explain why I didn't like that game.

My own favourite exhibit is a little house—a shack really—with only three walls. Here speakers pump out the sound of a woman singing. Her voice has a hopeful lilt, and in the background, a baby cries. When I peer into this room full of grit and coarse wool, its fluorescent half-shell open to all sorts of false memories, I always feel like I can taste mud. I try to remember if I was once this woman, if she begat me. The truth is, I am a latecomer to this land, with little heritage to claim. Still, I know the shape of no other shore, so perhaps it is the coming and going, rather than the dwelling, to which I can attach. Or maybe it is something else, something missing from the tired carpet surrounding this display … the green things, the growing things, the soil that can be dug and redug, by anyone.

We had owned our house for less than a year when I got my bees. Vegetable beds, fruit trees, berry patches. Rhododendrons, roses and a swathe of native plantings down the slope. Our purchase was the fulfilment of privilege and an attempt to future-proof our family in an uncertain world. On the day I was installing the hives, a neighbour I had never met turned up, curious and insistent. It turned out he also kept bees. 'Keep an eye out for wasps, will you?' he said. Wasps attack the bees and threaten the hive, he explained. I solemnly promised to keep watch. Sure enough, a few weeks later, I saw a wasp flying away from my hive, locked in a death struggle with one of my bees. Later, I watched the little workers fighting another narrow yellow body on the ground in front of the hive. I had always trodden carefully there. But that day, I put my foot down in anger.

In New Zealand we are trained young with a hatred for certain living things. Not all living things, of course. We have careful scripts through which we learn to hate possums and stoats and love fat, helpless ground birds. Later, if we take an interest in gardening, we enter into debates about what constitutes a weed and, thus, which flowers to find beautiful. So much of the national identity is tied to our geographic and ecological context; the fragile ecosystems that introduced species have almost destroyed. Much of our national consciousness centres on isolation, protection, and perhaps exclusion. There are parallels between ecological colonisation and the social and cultural devastation that tangata whenua also lived through. Yet conservation thinking may not provide a helpful roadmap for bicultural nationhood.

We cannot box up settlers and send them home. In some countries, this is a realistic model of decolonisation, but here Pākehā dwell under the protection of Te Tiriti (honoured consistently by tangata whenua, even when dishonoured by others). Still, it is easier to be Pākehā if we see ourselves as productive, not destructive—if instead of stoats or rabbits, we can be bees. After all, the honeybee is our most productive settler—an introduced organism that is effectively pollinating native plants alongside introduced ones. In this way and more, they represent new patterns of biointimacy forged between people and the environment. It isn't just about honey either—European bee species were soon recognised as essential to the white clover sown far and wide with seeds from 'the homeland'. The clover took happily to its new soil but couldn't reseed without a pollinator. Today great depilated swatches of the nation roll thick with clover. In the Mackenzie Country, where my husband's family have farmed for four generations, massive intensive irrigation systems make green what is, ecologically speaking, a desert. And so, while bees are not a pest, neither are they innocent. A butterfly flaps its wings and causes a hurricane; a bee flaps its wings and causes a wave of colonial land practices, full of intensive monocrops and chemical supplements, indigenous dispossession and threatened traditional knowledge. Things grow—but which things? The land changes forever.

Part Three: The Bees

It is easier to labour with someone at your side. When working in the garden, I often talk to my bees. 'How are you doing today, busy girls?' Once my daughter, close at my side, piped up: 'And boys too, Mum!'. Actually, these foragers are all female, I explained to her. A smaller number of male drone bees are inside the hive but they don't often come out willingly. I know this because a couple of weeks after getting my hive, I saw a large bee stumbling around just outside the entrance. I watched, I worried, and I googled. I attached pictures to an anxious email sent to the beekeeper who had delivered them. 'Is this my queen, wandering about? She doesn't look well.' Not the queen, but a male drone, he explained. At this time of year, the females kick them out of the hive. 'It's hard to be a male!' he finished his reply. Over the next few weeks, I watched more thick-bodied drones wobble around the bark chips in the cooling autumn air. They died there, or sometimes inside—their bodies dragged out of the entrance by others, a monument to efficiency. But death comes to all, and soon the ground was littered with the bodies of female workers, too; numbers inside the hive were dropping. This was all part of a natural process, to pick up again in spring, yet I found it disconcerting. After years of proudly saving exhausted bees from footpaths, I worked hard to stifle my pity.

*

All the bees have a role in making the honey. My only role is to take. In a few months, the man in the white truck will return to do the harvesting and processing, then bring it back to me in jars: valuable stuff nowadays. This honey will be 'multi-floral'—derived from a mishmash of suburban garden fodder and mānuka from the bush-covered hills behind. But *pure* mānuka honey, especially, makes big money. Now globally recognised for its medicinal qualities, there has been a flurry to protect the name on the global market. Honey has to be formally tested for four chemical markers to be labelled for export.

At the end of the day when I'm tired from office work, or the garden, I tuck myself and the kids under a blanket on the couch. The TV comes to life before us: we have been watching *Honey Wars,* a New Zealand reality show about a Māori-owned honey business in Northland. Māori were some of the first commercial beekeepers in the country. By the time Mary took her hives away from Māngungu, honeybees had already spread into the forests; they were ubiquitous and feral. By the 1860s, there were nests throughout the North Island bush. Reverend William Cotton's famous book about beekeeping, published in 1849, was one of the earliest books translated into Māori. Honey became taonga, incorporated into existing systems of indigenous science and healing. A century and a half later, when scientists eventually came to explain the health benefits of mānuka honey to them, they laughed: 'Our tupuna (ancestors) have known and shared this rongoa (traditional Māori medicine) for generations', they told him.

Many people have made money from honey gathered on Māori land. By the 1920s, there were over 100,000 hives recorded across New Zealand. The industry flourished even more after World War II, by which time there were over 7000 beekeepers and 150,000 hives. One famous beekeeper's son left to stake his own 'first' on a different mountain. He got his $5 note. Mary's bees were the start of a $5 billion industry for New Zealand. Amid the big corporations, Māori-owned honey businesses have persisted—sometimes growing into multimillion-dollar iwi-run operations, whose managers recall learning the process for smoking wild bees out from rock nests from their parents and grandparents.

*

After 2006, beekeeping became an especially valuable and tenuous profession. This was the year the Western world learned to appreciate bees to a new degree. It was a lesson learned through loss. Colony collapse disorder spread throughout the world with no clear explanation. Alongside growing awareness of climate change, there was sudden attention to the essential role of bees in supporting farming production, crop growth, and life in general—the interconnectedness of things, which indigenous groups have long understood. And so it is that bees have settled into our collective consciousness anew—an emblem of the Anthropocene, needed now more than ever as we continue to burn the cold white candle of the world at both ends, to smoke ourselves to sleep in the cities. 'Saving the bees' became a political act. Even in respectable suburbia, an unmown berm is forgiven. It is for this reason, and more, that I stand in my garden and feel undeservedly satisfied, watching my bees.

Sometimes it feels like they are stitching together a land patchworked by colonial greed, hunger, hubris. But that would be too easy, and colonisation is not a story to be told only in the past tense.

Concluding my search for the good settler

Twenty-four years after arriving in Hokianga, Mary Bumby once more boarded a ship. It was 1863 and she and Gideon were returning to England to settle their daughters into boarding school—another five-month journey, no salt-sick bees to worry over this time. But Mary's lungs carried their own bacterial spectres—known then as 'consumption'—and halfway through their journey, in stormy weather, Mary grew ill and died.

When the sun came out, they carried her body up to the deck. You can imagine it, can't you? The light on the green, green ocean, as her family and the crew gathered to say goodbye. Perhaps her soul buzzed and whirled above the water for a while, disoriented in the space between two homes. Maybe there was a paradise already waiting—one not of her own making, and needing no bees to flourish. But it is a pity to think of a garden without bees. Because bees are not only what they are. They are a symbol and a feeling, sweet and sharp, fertile and familiar. Knowing this, I know also that I have risked turning Mary Bumby into something more than herself; her story serving as a landing pad for my own frustrated and mobile hopes. But stories that are truly about transformation rely on honesty about things often misremembered. So I sit with my own history, and hers, and try to be honest for both our sakes.

Sometimes I still wake in the middle of night's ocean with my thoughts abuzz—searching for a direction, for a good settler to show me the way. But in the full light of day, I know that the good settler is a myth and that I exist in this land not by my own moral merit but through the tender circuits of promise, privilege and law. The transformation, the restoration that I would like to be a part of, starts with something more simple than sweat: with recognition of place, and a sense of belonging. So, I am left with nothing to do but send up a silent prayer that all of the futures we have killed on this passage to tomorrow have a garden at their end. And then go out into the garden and stand, and see, and learn.

REFERENCES

Twelve years prior … Cliff Van Eaton, *Mānuka: The biography of an extraordinary honey* (Exisle Publishing, 2014).

the curiosity of the Maoris … Peter Barrett, *The Immigrant Bees, 1788 to 1898: A cyclopaedia on the introduction of European honeybees into Australia and New Zealand* (Springwood, NSW: 1995).

sleeping in the cold and greedy sea … Anne Middleditch and David F. Bumby, *Mary Bumby: The first person to take honeybees to New Zealand* (Northern Bee Books, 2018).

spent too much time helping … Ibid.

In some countries … Ocean Ripeka Mercier, 'What is decolonisation?' in *Imagining Decolonisation* (BWB Texts, 2020).

The clover took happily … Allan Gillingham, 'Beekeeping: First bees and early beekeeping', *Te Ara – the Encyclopedia of New Zealand*: www.teara.govt.nz/en/beekeeping/page-1

Māori were some of the first … 'Honey bees brought to New Zealand', New Zealand History: https://nzhistory.govt.nz/mary-bumby-brings-the-first-honey-bees-in-new-zealand

our tupuna … Gillingham, 'Beekeeping'.

Many people have made … Lee Umbers, 'Northland iwi turns family pastime into million dollar mānuka honey operation', *Stuff*, 30 April 2017: www.stuff.co.nz/business/91931617/northland-iwi-turns-family-pastime-into-multimillion-dollar-mānuka-honey-operation

there were over 7000 beekeepers … Gillingham, 'Beekeeping'.

Mary's bees were the start … Apiculture New Zealand, 'Our industry': https://apinz.org.nz/about/#:~:text=New%20Zealand's%20apiculture%20industry%20is,our%20agricultural%20and%20horticultural%20sectors

whose managers recall … Umbers, 'Northland iwi'.

not a story to be told … Moana Jackson, 'Where to next? Decolonisation and the stories of the land' in *Imagining Decolonisation* (BWB Texts, 2020).

About the Selecting Editors

Lynley Edmeades is a poet, essayist and academic. She is the author of three books: *As the Verb Tenses* (Otago University Press, 2016), *Listening In* (Otago University Press, 2019) and *Bordering on Miraculous* (Massey University Press, 2022). In 2017 she was the Ursula Bethell Writer in Residence at the University of Canterbury and the Artist in Residence at Massey University. She has a PhD in avant-garde poetics, and her scholarship on Gertrude Stein and John Cage has been published internationally. She lives in Ōtepoti where she teaches creative writing at the University of Otago. She is currently working on a book-length essay project and is the present editor of *Landfall*.

Emma Neale is the author or selecting editor of over fourteen titles. She has had her writing short-listed, long-listed or placed in a number of national and international awards, including the Ockham New Zealand Book Awards, the Dublin International Literary Award, the Bridport Prize, the Bath Flash Fiction Award, the Kathleen Grattan Award and the Fish Publishing Short Story Award. In 2020, she received the Lauris Edmond Memorial Award for a Distinguished Contribution to New Zealand Poetry. Her novel, *Fosterling* (Penguin Random House, 2011) is in script development with Sandy Lane Productions, under the title *Skin*. She works in Ōtepoti as an editor.

Contributor Biographies

Tīhema Baker (Raukawa te Au ki te Tonga, Ātiawa ki Whakarongotai, Ngāti Toa Rangatira) is a writer from Ōtaki on the Kāpiti Coast. He holds a master's in Creative Writing and is the author of the satirical novel *Turncoat*, the YA series *The Watchers Trilogy* and various short stories.

Maddie Ballard is a Chinese-Pākehā writer from Tāmaki Makaurau. She is undertaking a master's in creative writing at the International Institute of Modern Letters. Her writing has appeared in *Starling*, *The Pantograph Punch* and *Turbine|Kapohau*.

Dr Rachel Buchanan (Taranaki, Te Ātiawa) is a historian, curator and speechwriter. Her new book, *Te Motunui Epa* (BWB Books, 2022), was shortlisted for the Ockham New Zealand Book Awards 2023, and won the Ernest Scott Prize for History in the same year.

Jayne Costelloe has been a technical writer in Wellington for over 20 years, and has turned to creative non-fiction and fiction writing.

Lynn Davidson's memoir *Do You Still Have Time for Chaos?* will be published by Te Herenga Waka University Press in 2024. Her latest poetry collection *Islander* was published by Shearsman Books and Te Herenga Waka University Press in 2019.

Andrew Dean is Lecturer in Writing and Literature at Deakin University, Victoria, Australia. He published *Metafiction and the Postwar Novel: Foes, ghosts, and faces in the water* with Oxford University Press in 2021. He is currently researching Jewish comedy and issues in psychoanalysis.

Charlotte Doyle is a non-fiction writer based in Te Whanganui-a-Tara. She completed a master's in Creative Writing at the International Institute of Modern Letters in 2021. Her writing, which tends to ask lots of questions, has been published in *takahē*, *Turbine|Kapohau* and *The Pantograph Punch*.

Jess Ducey (they/them) is a Wellingtonian now living in New York City. Jess enjoys nature, queer art, knitting, dinner parties, books, public transit, cheese, bikes and patting other people's dogs. Their writing has previously appeared on RNZ National.

Susanna Elliffe is a word-lover from Ōamaru. Susanna is a perennial student with a BA in English Literature (VUW) and a Graduate Diploma in Creative Writing (Massey). She has spent most of her life playing with words. Shortlisted for the Bridport Prize in 2022, Susanna has been highly commended in the *Sunday Star Times*, Sargeson Prize and Landfall Essay Competition (2019, 2020 and 2021).

Bonnie Etherington is Lecturer in Literary and Creative Communication at Te Herenga Waka Victoria University of Wellington, and from 2020–2021 was the CU Boulder Environmental Futures Postdoctoral Fellow. Bonnie was born in Aotearoa New Zealand and raised in West Papua.

Dr Norman P. Franke is a New Zealand-based poet, scholar and documentary filmmaker. He has published widely about eighteenth-century literature and German-speaking exile literature (Albert Einstein, Else Lasker-Schüler, Karl Wolfskehl) and eco-poetics. His poetry has been broadcast on radio and published in anthologies in Austria, Germany, New Zealand, Switzerland, the UK and the US.

Sarah Harpur Ruigrok (Kāi Tahu: Kāti Huirapa, Kāti Hāwea, Kāi Te Ruahikihiki) is an award-winning playwright and performer. She's written and performed six solo shows at local and international festivals. She works in communications and lives on the Kāpiti Coast with her husband, son and two annoying dogs.

Gill James is a former public sector lawyer and law drafter who has always wanted to write creatively. She grew up in Christchurch but has lived in Wellington most of her life. She is in her second year studying for a master's in Creative Writing at Massey University.

Claire Mabey is a writer, books editor at The Spinoff, founder of Verb Wellington and mum to Charlie. She writes a sporadic newsletter at clairemabey.substack.com and is currently working on a novel.

Tina Makereti, author of *The Imaginary Lives of James Pōneke* and *Where the Rēkohu Bone Sings*, is working on a collection of personal essays and a novel. In 2016 her story 'Black Milk' won the Commonwealth Writers Short Story Prize, Pacific region. She teaches creative writing at the IIML, Te Herenga Waka Victoria University of Wellington.

Alexis O'Connell completed a master's in Creative Writing at the University of Canterbury. She has been an HOD of English and now co-owns an advisory business.

Maggie Sturgess resides in Te Whanganui-a-Tara where she works as a clinical psychologist and writer.

Susan Wardell is an academic and writer from Ōtepoti. She has been nationally and internationally awarded for poetry, flash fiction and essays. Susan teaches and researches social anthropology at the University of Otago, often using creative writing to explore her academic interests through more personal, autoethnographic or humanistic registers.